CLOUD COMPUTING - TECHNOLOGY AND PRACTICES

Edited by **Dinesh G. Harkut, Kashmira N. Kasat** and **Saurabh A. Shah**

Cloud Computing - Technology and Practices
http://dx.doi.org/10.5772/intechopen.72088
Edited by Dinesh G. Harkut, Kashmira N. Kasat and Saurabh A. Shah

Contributors

Alexey Bataev, Eghbal Ghazizadeh, Brian Cusack, Chien Wen Hung, Isaac Ayodeji Odun-Ayo, Dinesh G. Harkut

Notice

First published in London, United Kingdom, 2019 by IntechOpen
IntechOpen is the global imprint of INTECHOPEN LIMITED, registered in England and Wales, registration number: 11086078, The Shard, 25th floor, 32 London Bridge Street
London, SE19SG – United Kingdom
Printed in Croatia

British Library Cataloguing-in-Publication Data
A catalogue record for this book is available from the British Library

Additional hard copies can be obtained from orders@intechopen.com

Cloud Computing - Technology and Practices, Edited by Dinesh G. Harkut, Kashmira N. Kasat and Saurabh A. Shah
p. cm.
Print ISBN 978-1-78984-915-8
Online ISBN 978-1-78984-916-5

For EU product safety concerns:
IN TECH d.o.o., Prolaz Marije Krucifikse Kozulić 3, 51000 Rijeka, Croatia,
info@intechopen.com or visit our website at intechopen.com.

Meet the editors

Dinesh G. Harkut is currently working as an Associate Professor at PRMCEAM, Badnera, India, in the Computer Science and Engineering Department. He obtained his Bachelors, Masters of Engineering Degree (CSE), and PhD (CSE) from Sant Gadge Baba Amravati University (SGBAU), Amravati University, Maharashtra, India. He has also obtained a Master's Degree and PhD in Business Administration. His primary research interests are in computer AI, big data, analytics, embedded systems, and e-commerce. He has supervised around 18 Master's Degree and 24 Bachelor's Degree students. He has published 40 papers in refereed journals and published three books with international publishers. He is having two patents filed and published in his name in India and has organized various workshops, sessions, conferences, and trainings. He is principal investigator in setting center of excellence of renowned technological giants like IBM, Oracle, Texas Instruments, and Huawei at PRMCEAM and establishing industry-funded laboratories from ARM, Cypress Semiconductor, Intel FPGA, Wind River, and Xilinx fetched a grant in the tune of Rs. 351.32 lacs.
He is a fellow member of the Institute of Electronics and Telecommunication Engineering (IETE), New Delhi, a life member of the Indian Society for Technical Education (ISTE), New Delhi, a senior member of the Universal Association of Computer and Electronics Engineers (UACEE), USA, and a professional member of the International Association of Engineers (IAENG), Hong Kong.

Dr. Ms. Kashmira N. Kasat received her Doctorate (PhD) Degree in Electronic Engineering from Sant Gadge Baba Amravati University (SGBAU) in 2017. She completed her Graduation B.E. (Industrial Electronics) from JNEC, Aurangabad, in 1999 and Postgraduation M.E. (Electronics) from GCOE, Aurangabad, in 2009. Presently she is working as head and assistant professor in the Electronics and Telecommunication Department. She has 12 years of teaching and industrial experience. She has published 17 papers in national/international journals and has also published a book *Computer Programming* with Pearson Publications, 2011. She has two patents filed and published under her belt. She has supervised 16 UG level 07 PG level projects. Her areas of research include power electronics, soft computing, and VLSI design. She is a life member of ISTE and IETE and senior member of the Universal Association of Computer and Electronics Engineers (UACEE). She is the editorial board member of the Scientific Board of Computer, Electrical and Electronic Engineers, International Institute of Engineers, UK.

Prof. Saurabh A. Shah, BE (Computer Engineering), ME (Computer Science and Engineering), has been working as an assistant professor in the Department of Computer Science and Engineering at Ram Meghe College of Engineering and Management, Badnera, since 2010. Currently, he is pursuing his PhD in Computer Science and Engineering at Sant Gadge Baba Amravati University. He has 9 years of experience in teaching at undergraduate level. He is a Life Member of the Indian Society for Technical Education and an Associate Member of the Institute of Electronics and Telecommunication Engineers. His areas of interest are cloud computing, image processing, and computer programming.

Contents

Preface

A good head and good heart are always a formidable combination.
But when you add to that a literate tongue or pen, then you have something very special.
—Nelson Mandela

This book covers the comprehensive introduction on Cloud Computing, the latest buzzword in the computing industry. Cloud computing is an emerging technology that enables access to shared resources and provides higher level services with minimal management effort. The globalization of computing assets may be the biggest contribution that cloud has made to date. The core concept of cloud computing is easy to understand when one explores what modern IT environments desire to achieve by dynamically enhancing the capabilities of existing infrastructure without investing or procuring new resources. Widespread application of cloud computing realizes the saving potential associated with the ability to outsource the software and hardware necessary for tech services. The emphasis is on insight and understanding, not just on formalisms. We have attempted to present the material in clear, simple style.

Dr. Dinesh G. Harkut, Dr. Kashmira N. Kasat, and Mr. Saurabh A. Shah
Prof Ram Mehge College of Engineering & Management
Badnera-Amravati, M.S., India

Chapter 1

Introductory Chapter: Cloud Computing

Dinesh G. Harkut

Additional information is available at the end of the chapter

http://dx.doi.org/10.5772/intechopen.81247

1. Introduction

Cloud computing has recently emerged as one of the latest buzzwords in the computing industry. It is the latest evolution of computing, where IT resources are offered as services. Cloud computing provides on-demand, scalable, device-independent, and reliable services to its users. Cloud computing is all the rage, allowing for the delivery of computing and storage capacity to a diverse community of end-recipients. Clouds are distributed technology platforms that leverage sophisticated technology innovations to provide highly scalable and resilient environments that can be remotely utilized by organizations in a multitude of powerful ways. Cloud computing differs from peer-to-peer, client-server, grid computing, virtualization, and its levels. Over time, the technologies have evolved and led to the development of cloud computing in a phase-wise manner:

- *Utility computing*: in this model, the provider of the services owns, operates, and manages the computing and other infrastructure, and the enterprise subscribers access it as and when required on a rental or metered basis or on-demand pay-per-use billing mode.
- *Computer cluster*: a group of linked computers, which work together in a closely coupled environment such that, in many respects, it appears that these computers form a single computer.
- *Grid computing*: network of various computer resources working in unison like a supercomputer to process and execute resource-hungry applications. It is a hardware architecture that associates various computer resources to reach a main objective. A grid works on various scientific or technical tasks that are too big for a supercomputer and require great number of computers processing power or access to large amount of data.
- *Cloud computing*: it relies on sharing computing resources instead of having dedicated local servers or personal devices to handle applications. It supports and facilitates dynamically scalable and often virtualized resources which are provided as a server over the Internet.

Cloud computing delivers IT services by facilitating the access of resources from the Internet through web-based tools and applications, as opposed to a direct connection to a server. Instead of storing the files on a proprietary hard drive or local storage device, cloud-based storage makes it possible to save them to a remote database over Internet. Internet connection is at the heart of cloud computing and devices having access to the Internet can only access the data and the software programs to run it. The phrase cloud computing derives as the information being accessed is found at virtual space—the cloud that allows its user to work remotely and enables the user to gain access to its service irrespective of the location. Companies extending cloud services enable users to store files and applications on remote servers, and then access all the data via the Internet. The Internet becomes the cloud, and your data, work, and applications are available from any device with which you can connect to the Internet, anywhere across world. The cloud-based services are accessible anywhere in the world, as long as Internet connection is available.

Cloud computing infrastructure consists of time-tested and highly reliable services built on servers with varying levels of virtualized technologies. Commercial offerings have evolved to meet the quality-of-service (QoS) requirements of customers and typically provide such service-level-agreement (SLA) to their customers. Customers generally do not own the infrastructure used in a cloud computing environment; they can forgo capital expenditure and consume resources as a service by just paying for what they use. Ultimately, cloud computing is likely to bring super-computing capabilities to the mass with bare minimum capital cost. Cloud computing enables multitenancy, which in turn enables sharing of resources and costs among a large pool of users. Centralization of resources in cloud computing environments lowers the cost of infrastructure and improves efficiency by dynamic allocation of CPU, storage, and network bandwidth. The use of multiple redundant sites in cloud computing results in higher reliability and higher dynamic scalabilities that vary as per the changing demands. Sustainability issues of cloud computing because of higher energy consumption at resource site are addressed by leveraging improvement in resource utilization and implementation of more energy-efficient systems.

The term cloud is often used as a metaphor for the Internet and can be defined as new type of utility computing that basically uses virtual servers that have been made available to third parties via the Internet. The cloud sees no borders and thus has made the world a much smaller place. The Internet is global in scope but respects only established communication paths. Globalization of computing assets may be the biggest contribution the cloud has made to date. For this reason, the cloud is the subject of many complex geopolitical issues.

The core concept of cloud computing becomes easy to understand when one begins to think and knows what the modern IT environments desire to achieve, which may vary from the mean to dynamically increase the capacity or add enhanced capabilities to their existing infrastructure, that too without investing money in procuring the new infrastructure, without even investing in training the manpower and without investing in upgrading licenses for new software. Cloud computing models that encompass a subscription-based or pay-per-use paradigm provide a service that can be used over the Internet and extend an IT shop's existing capabilities.

Cloud computing market is becoming increasingly crowded over time. Major players in this domain are Amazon, Aliyun, Google, IBM Bluemix, Microsoft, Salesforce, and Sun, having different focus areas and offerings. Offerings vary from generalized infrastructure related to servers, storage bandwidth, databases, Web services, and developer platforms to more specific services related to CRM, HR, and security. Offerings also vary from vendor to vender – Amazon offers purely pay-per-use public outsource model, Google Cloud focuses on consumer banking and retail, whereas Microsoft Azure the latest entrant offers data centers and allows clients to keep some data at their own sites. Customer base is varying from big enterprises to small and medium-size business establishments. Different business corporates can employ cloud computing in different ways. Some users maintain all apps and data on the cloud, while others use a hybrid model, keeping certain apps and data on private servers and others on the cloud.

In order to have better understanding of how computing has evolved, it is imperative to know and understand the evolution of computing from a historical perspective which focuses primarily on those advances that led to the development of cloud computing, such as the transition from mainframes to desktop, laptops, and mobile devices on the cloud. When it comes to offering technology in pay-as-you-use service model, most information technology professionals have heard it all—from allocated resource management to grid computing, to on-demand computing and to utility computing. Computer time-sharing computing technology might lead to a future where computing power and even specific applications might be sold through a utility-type business model. Utility can be defined as the provision of computational and storage resources as metered service, similar to those provided by a traditional public utility company. There is a paradigm shift as far as adoption and acceptance of cloud technology are concerned. As trust and reliability issues are resolved, enterprises are showing more faith and confidence and have started to hire services which are even more critical and sensitive like virtual servers that IT departments and users can access on demand as it was confined to only non-mission-critical needs.

Cloud computing extends subscription-based access to infrastructure, platforms, and applications that are popularly referred to as IaaS (Infrastructure as a Service), PaaS (Platform as a Service), and SaaS (Software as a Service).

- *Software as a Service* (*SaaS*): the focus for SaaS is on the end user as opposed to managed services and involves the licensure of a software application to customers. Licenses are typically provided through a pay-as-you-go model or on-demand.
- *Infrastructure as a Service* (*IaaS*): clients can avoid the need to purchase software or servers, and instead procure these resources in an outsourced and on-demand service mode. It involves delivering everything from operating systems to servers and storage through IP-based connectivity as part of an on-demand service.
- *Platform as a Service* (*PaaS*): PaaS is a variation of SaaS, wherein the platform is deliverable rather than application and is considered the most complex as compared to SaaS and IaaS. Unlike SaaS, which delivers software online, here, a platform for creating software is delivered.

Indeed, cloud computing has enabled and paved ways for increased interoperability and usability by reducing the cost of computation, data storage and delivery, and application hosting significantly. To achieve consistent and reliable operation under peak loads which is at the core of cloud technology, the cost and complexity involved in ensuring that applications and services can scale as needed are significantly high.

1.1. Advantages of cloud computing

- *Reliability*: cloud computing is much more reliable and consistent than in-house IT infrastructure as it is managed by expert service providers and bounded by service level agreement, which guarantees reliability and availability that is supported by a massive pool of redundant IT resources maintained by the service provider.
- *Data recovery*: in case of crash, recovery of data either from proprietary or local storage becomes tedious or a costly affair. Instead, professionally managed cloud computing providers enable automatic data backup on the cloud system as they are having redundant storage and are typically supervised by the domain experts.
- *Manageability*: cloud computing provides enhanced maintenance capabilities through central administration of resources, vendor-managed infrastructure, and SLA-backed agreements. Clients enjoy a simple web-based user interface for accessing software, applications, and services—without owning it and an SLA ensures the timely and guaranteed delivery, management, and maintenance of clients' IT services.
- *Data centralization*: another key benefit of cloud services is the centralized data. The information for multiple projects and different branch offices is stored in one location that can be accessed from remote places.
- *Cost savings*: the most significant benefit of cloud computing is cost savings. Irrespective of business type or size, cloud computing saves substantial capital cost and operational expenses. The lack of on-premises infrastructure also removes their associated operational costs in the form of power, air conditioning, and administration costs. Apart from large business organizations, cloud services are extremely affordable for smaller businesses.
- *Device independence*: no need to stick to single computer or network.
- *Strategic edge*: timely updated latest computing resources give you a competitive edge over competitors, as the updated IT procurement time is virtually nil and thus allows clients to forget about technology and focus on their key business activities and objectives. Clients can deploy mission-critical applications that deliver significant business benefits, without any upfront costs and minimal provisioning time.

1.2. Disadvantages of cloud computing

- *Uptime*: as Internet connection is the lifeline of cloud computing, if your Internet connection is offline, the client will not be able to access any of your applications, server, or data from the cloud. As cloud service providers take care of a number of clients each day, they can become overwhelmed and may even come up against technical outages. This can lead to client business processes being temporarily suspended.

- *Low bandwidth*: with a low-bandwidth net, the benefits of cloud computing cannot be utilized. Sometimes, even a high-bandwidth satellite connection can lead to poor quality performance due to high latency.
- *Security issues*: the very intrinsic nature of clouds makes it a soft target for hackers as it hosts services to various clients and thus the business can become vulnerable to hackers and threats. Security is the measure area of concern when opting for cloud-powered technologies as it involves giving access to sensitive data and business logics in third-party service provider. This risk can be mitigated by adopting and implementing the best, trusted, and tested security measures and standards while storing data and important files on external service providers.
- *Host lock-in*: although cloud service providers promise that the cloud will be flexible to use and integrate, switching cloud services is a very hectic task. Organizations may find it difficult to migrate from one vendor to another. Hosting and integrating current cloud applications on another platform may throw up interoperability and support issues.
- *Limited flexibility*: enterprises hiring cloud computing services are having limited control over the functions of the software as well as hardware as application and services run on a remote server. As applications always run on remote software, it provides the very minimal flexibility to the users.
- *Minimal control*: third-party service provider owns, manages, and monitors the infrastructure and relives the customer from all housekeeping tasks. Thus, the customer is free to concentrate and focus entirely on controlling and managing the applications, data, and services operated on top of that, not the back-end infrastructure itself.
- *Incompatibility*: sometimes, there are problems of software incompatibility, as some applications, tools, and software connect particularly to a personal computer.

Technological advancement and ease of use have made cloud as an integral and mandatory part of every business venture. There are pros and cons of cloud but one cannot think without enjoying the benefits of cloud computing as strategically planned use of cloud service can minimize the disadvantages of cloud computing. Furthermore, latest precautionary and security measures can enhance the reliability of the services offered by cloud. Cloud computing has rocked the business world as it harnesses the benefit through minimized costs, easy access, data backup, data centralization, sharing capabilities, security, free storage, and quick testing. The argument becomes even stronger with their enhanced flexibility and dependability.

2. Challenges in cloud computing

A major problem that needs to be addressed in all the cases is that of availability of services and security.

Security of data, high-speed Internet, and standardization are the major challenges associated with cloud computing. Legal framework needs to be in place as far as protection of users' identity, privacy, and application-specific data. Secondly, without high-speed Internet connection, true benefits of cloud computing are untenable. Because of the varied nature of cloud computing, i.e., set of centralized resources used by mass, it is mandatory to have some protocol and technical standardization in place to facilitate its easy and seamless widespread adoption and make it a mainstream method of computing for the mass.

Infrastructure security, data security and storage, identity and access management, security management and privacy are the various sensitive fronts from security perspectives that need to be addressed. Cloud service provider needs to play a very vital role in providing the utmost security with greater transparency. Greater transparency needs to be complimented by significantly enhanced and improved security technology which is needed in both preventive controls and detective controls. Cloud computing is a low-cost solution that offers responsiveness and flexibility with ease. The role of the corporate IR departments is impacted significantly by the adaptations of cloud computing as it provides cost-effective solutions. A major share of annual budgets of majority of IT departments is allocated to maintenance and depreciation of the resources without any value addition. This diminished view of IT's value directly to business units is reinforced by cloud computing's pay-as-you-go business model and the shift from capital expenditure to operational expenditure.

The cloud computing environment presents new challenges from an audit and compliance perspective, but much can be used from traditional outsourcing models. To support internal business and risk management objectives and to support customer requirements, it is essential for cloud service providers to identify the requirements with which it must abide. Though audit and compliance functions played an important role in traditional outsourcing relationships, the dynamic nature of cloud computing services demands increased importance and attention. It is imperative that the cloud service provider must take a programmatic approach to monitor and regulate these compliance and support customer requirements.

3. Conclusion

One of the biggest impediments to cloud computing has been Internet bandwidth. With the advent of superfast, 3G and 4G wireless technology, widespread adoptions of broadband services, stringent Internet security standards, and protocols exporting huge data clusters out of their buildings and into someone else's hands have become more safe and fast. Widespread application of cloud computing realizes the savings potential associated with the ability to outsource the software and hardware necessary for tech services.

Author details

Dinesh G. Harkut

Address all correspondence to: dg.harkut@gmail.com

Department of Computer Science and Engineering, Prof Ram Meghe College of Engineering and Management, Badnera, M.S., India

Chapter 2

Cloud Computing

Chien Wen Hung

Additional information is available at the end of the chapter

http://dx.doi.org/10.5772/intechopen.77283

Abstract

Cloud computing was a cloud technology pioneered by Amazon for a long time due to its software technology that is based on the online shopping platform. After Google, Microsoft also follow up, and this technology, in fact, already exists in our lives, and applications continue to expand, become an integral part of life. With the rapid development of the Internet and the demand for high-speed computing of mobile devices, the simplest cloud computing technology has been widely used in online services, such as "search engine, webmail," and so on. Users can get a lot of information by simply entering a simple instruction. Further cloud computing is not only for data search and analysis function, but also can be used in the biological sciences, such as: analysis of cancer cells, analysis of DNA structure, gene mapping sequencing; in the future more Smart phone, GPS and other mobile devices through the cloud computing to develop more application service.

Keywords: cloud technology, smart phone, GPS

1. Introduction

As early as 1983, Sun Computer proposed the concept of "network as a computer", opening up the direction of thinking and development.

In 2006, Amazon introduced "resilient cloud services" and decentralized architecture technologies to provide limited-service web services.

In 2006, Eric Schmidt, Google's chief executive, put forward the concept of "cloud computing," laying another new era in computer development.

In 2007, Google and IBM, in cooperation with prestigious universities in the United States, started to develop "Cloud Services" software and hardware technology on campus and provided school professors and students to develop large-scale research projects on the Internet.

In 2008, Yahoo, Hewlett-Packard, Intel and the United States, Germany and Singapore jointly launched a large-scale research and development platform for cloud computing to build 6 data center research centers. On average, each data center is equipped with 2500 processors and is actively developing cloud service technologies.

In 2008, Dell officially applied to the U.S. Patent and Trademark Office for a "cloud computing" patent application. In the meantime, large names such as Fujitsu, Red Hat, Hewlett Packard, IBM, VMware, and NetApp compete in R & D.

In 2010, NASA teamed up with major computer vendors such as Rackspace, AMD, Intel, Dell and Microsoft to develop cloud computing technologies.

The meaning of cloud computing is to store the data stored in the local computer and store it in the cloud website. The calculation is made by the local computer and handed over to the cloud computing website. Users do not need to worry about hardware devices, system installation, applications, just open the cloud page, you can perform various types of data storage and computing.

The basic characteristic of cloud computing is "computing in the cloud", that is, building a large-scale data center by combining multiple useful websites to satisfy any data storage and problem computing; meanwhile, users are not required to worry about their own hardware and software facilities. Cloud site consider all possible troubles. As long as the user open the web page, send information to complete the operation.

Cloud computing can be described as "network computer", make full use of the Internet function to connect multiple useful sites, the formation of cloud sites, providing users with data storage and problem computing; users no longer worry about local storage devices and computing applications, do not have to worry about computer professional knowledge, through the Internet to connect to the cloud site, you can send data to the cloud storage page, the cloud application can solve the problem.

2. Cloud computing features

The basic characteristics of cloud computing is "computing in the cloud," that is, to meet:

1. Multiple large-scale data centers and a large number of processors: the combination of a number of useful websites and a large number of large-scale data centers and a large number of processors to meet any data storage and problem computing.

2. Cloud service: users do not need to worry about hardware devices, no troubles to install the system, no need to worry about applications, cloud sites consider all possible troubles, design execution web pages, users can simply open web pages to store data, computing data, delivery data.

If you want to create an all-encompassing cloud site, in some functional environment may be a waste of time, in order to properly apply, we can cloud site as:

1. Public cloud: public cloud is the most common way to deploy cloud computing. Cloud resources are owned and operated by third-party cloud service providers and delivered over the Internet. In the public cloud, all hardware, software, and other supported infrastructure is owned and managed by the cloud provider. In the public cloud, you share the same hardware, storage, and networking devices with other organizations or cloud rental users. You use a web browser to access services and manage your account. Common cloud deployments are commonly used to provide web-based email, online office applications, storage, and test and development environments.

   Public cloud benefits:

   a. Low cost—no need to purchase hardware or software, just pay for the services you use.

   b. No maintenance—maintenance is provided by service providers.

   c. Scalability—unlimited on demand to meet your business needs.

   d. High reliability—a wide range of server networks to ensure that from failure.

2. Private cloud: private clouds are comprised of cloud computing resources that are used exclusively by a single organization or organization. Private clouds can be physically located within the organization's local data center or hosted by third-party service providers. But in the private cloud, services and infrastructure are all maintained on the private network, with hardware and software exclusive to your organization. In this way, the private cloud enables organizations to more easily customize their resources to meet specific IT needs. Private clouds are widely adopted by government agencies, financial institutions, and other medium- and large-scale organizations that need to handle business-critical operations in pursuit of better control of their environment.

   The advantages of private cloud:

   a. More flexibility—your organization can customize the cloud environment to meet specific business needs.

   b. Improved security—no sharing of resources with other people, resulting in greater levels of control and security.

   c. High scalability—private clouds can still afford the scalability and efficiency of public clouds.

3. Hybrid cloud: combining both private and public clouds gives organizations the best of both worlds. In hybrid cloud, data and applications move between private and public clouds, making your enterprise more resilient and have more deployment options. For example, you can use a large number of projects with low security requirements (such as web-based email) for the public cloud, and use confidential, business-critical items such as

financial reports for private cloud (or other on-premises basic structure). In hybrid cloud, you can also choose Cloud Load Balancing. This is when an application or resource is executing in a private cloud until demand increases (such as seasonal activities such as online shopping or tax returns), during which time an organization can "load balance" the public cloud to apply other operations Resources.

The advantages of hybrid cloud:

a. Control—your organization can maintain the private infrastructure of confidential assets.

b. Resiliency—you can take full advantage of other resources in the public cloud, if needed.

c. Cost-effective—you can take advantage of changes to the public cloud to pay for additional computing power only when you need it.

d. Easily-switch to the cloud with less effort because you can move in and out-gradually introducing workload over time.

3. Cloud computing advantages and disadvantages

Cloud computing advantages [4].

1. In R & D and maintenance, because of the huge resources, the solution to the problem can be rapidly established and deployed to reduce the barriers of information problems and save the R & D and maintenance costs of new methods.

2. In terms of exchanging messages, users find problems and solve problems. Because cloud terminals are hubs, users can easily communicate with each other and exchange views with each other so that they can collaborate to solve problems and give play to their wisdom and ability.

3. In terms of slim and light development, users do not need to have large memory capacity and powerful computing functions, such as tablets and mobile phones, because of data storage and functional computing in the cloud.

4. In the system update, due to functional hardware and software are in the cloud site, where there is a newly developed system software, as long as the site updated, immediately put into use, users no longer have to worry about update and installation problems.

5. In terms of functional applications, it is easy to meet the needs of users by combining multiple useful websites with diverse functional backgrounds, providing highly competitive application functions and enhancing users' application capabilities and vendor reputation.

6. In terms of ease of use, cloud computing is a fast service, and users can operate anytime, anywhere as long as they are in an Internet-enabled area and open a webpage.

Cloud computing disadvantages [4].

1. There must be network connectivity between the cloud website and the user. Therefore, users in the area without the network cannot share any cloud function. If the network speed is slow, it will also affect the efficiency of the function and cannot handle difficult problems.
2. In order to build a cloud website, in addition to requiring huge funding, more personnel and equipment are needed. In the future, maintenance requires funds and talents. So running a cloud site has a very heavy burden on it.
3. Cloud computing is a new era of computer technology, and we are now using computer systems and methods, but also after a long time to build a little bit by bit, if you immediately give up straight to the cloud, will waste the previous investment; if not updated system will not keep up with new technology.
4. For users, participation in cloud computing can make the operation easy and effective, but it may also be a commercial trap. Once it enters the cloud, it will abandon its own capabilities and devices if it relies on the cloud. If the cloud system aggravates the payment, at this time can only be allowed to ask.

4. Cloud application status

Cloud computing industry can be divided into three categories: cloud software, cloud platform, cloud devices.

1. Cloud software (SaaS): to break the monopoly of the previous situation of manufacturers design, interested parties can develop their own design, propose a wide range of software services.
2. Cloud platform (PaaS): research and develop operating system platform, provide software developers to design cloud software and serve the general public via the Internet. As a result, operating system platforms and non-manufacturers with ample human and material resources cannot afford to participate. Currently, there are: Google, Yahoo!, Microsoft, Apple.
3. Cloud equipment (IaaS): the basic equipment (such as IT systems, databases, etc.) are systematically integrated to make it work together to provide the maximum storage space for data and provide the fastest execution time for the operation. The current participants: IBM, Dell, Sun, Hewlett-Packard, Amazon.

Enterprises in cloud service environment providing customized customer service have become popular. However, quick and proper understanding of customer needs to provide customized services should be a priority of companies. Therefore, the proposed customer service for customized applications and the use of data mining techniques to collect information from a large number of promotional products to meet customer needs will result in proactive customized information to the customer to save time searching for products. The system can enhance the competitiveness of enterprises and increase corporate profits.

1. SaaS is a model that provides software through the Internet. Instead of purchasing software, users can use the Web-based software to manage their business activities without having to maintain the software. The service provider manages and maintains the software, for many small businesses, SaaS is the best way to adopt advanced technology, which eliminates the need for companies to buy, build and maintain infrastructure and applications. In recent years, the rise of SaaS has given traditional packaged software vendors real pressure.

2. PaaS is a platform as a service (Platform as a service). Platform as a service is a cloud computing service that provides a computing platform and a solution stack as a service. At the typical level of cloud computing, the platform as a service layer is between software as a service and infrastructure as a service.

   Platform-as-a-service provides the ability for users to deploy and create cloud infrastructure to clients, or to use programming languages, libraries, and services. Users do not need to manage and control the cloud infrastructure, including the network, servers, operating systems or storage, but need to control the upper application deployment and application hosting environment.

   PaaS takes the software development platform as a service and delivers it to the user as a softwareas-a-service (SaaS) model. Therefore, PaaS is also an application of the SaaS model. However, the emergence of PaaS can accelerate the development of SaaS, especially to accelerate the development of SaaS application speed.

3. Infrastructure as a service (IaaS) is the software that consumers use to process, store, network and various basic computing resources, deploy and execute operating systems or applications, and so on. Clients can deploy and run processing, storage, networking, and other basic computing resources at will, without the need to purchase network devices such as servers and software. They cannot control or control the underlying infrastructure, but can control operating systems, storage devices, deployed applications.

5. Cloud platform

5.1. Google Cloud platform

Google (Google) to develop Gmail, Google Docs, Google Talk, iGoogle, Google Calendar and other online applications, the establishment of basic cloud computing platform. General users use the browser to connect to the designated website platform, you can edit the file, and then online archive. In the company did not complete the file, go home from work can be connected to the Internet to continue, Google Spreadsheet graphical online spreadsheets can be defined formula fill in the numerical calculation, Google Cloud Computing website, these work has nothing to do with the performance of the computer we use Only the internet connection speed is a problem.

In order for cloud sites to process large numbers of users and large amounts of information in parallel. The Google Cloud assumes that every information system can fail at any time, so use software layers to create fault tolerance and standardize machines. As the amount of data increases, the performance of the cloud system can only be achieved by continuously expanding the number of machines and equipment without modifying the original application. For example, the software layer includes three technologies: Google File System (GFS), distributed database Google BigTable (GBT), and Google MapReduce (GMR).

Google has been successfully developed and welcomed by users of the cloud site:

a. Gmail: each account provides 15 GB of high-capacity storage space, effectively control spam and provide normal operation assurance and security.

b. Google Calendar: a web-based calendar application that increases the productivity of individuals or groups of users, helps reduce the cost of work, and enhances the division of labor. Agenda management, scheduling, sharing of online calendar and calendar synchronization move.

c. Google Docs: provides the execution environment for word processing, trial execution, briefing and processing at anytime and anywhere, supports up to 1G unlimited file types upload (virtual hard disk) and instant sharing. Through the webpage, users are provided multiplayer editing files at the same time.

d. Google Talk: groups effectively interact and communicate, provide group mail communication, facilitate content sharing, and quickly search for files. Share calendars, documents, websites and videos.

e. Google Group: the joint vertical and horizontal integration of the intranet, the establishment of a safe and effective community team project.

f. Security: provide the best security solutions such as video, private files.

5.2. Yahoo Cloud platform

Yahoo! successfully developed four major technologies for cloud infrastructure:

a. Establishing cloud storage for structured and unstructured data.

b. Establishing large-scale decentralized data computing and storage.

c. Providing cloud data cache and proxy Function.

d. To provide advanced rapid data processing services.

The ultimate goal is to complete Online Serving, so that developers can complete the development environment online to establish and accelerate product and service development time.

Working with the Apache Software Foundation to develop Hadoop, a cloud-based operating system, Hadoop is a distributed computing environment written in Java that provides a wealth of data. Hadoop's architecture is based on the concept of BigTable and Google File System It is similar to the cloud computing architecture used internally by Google.

5.3. Microsoft Cloud platform

On the cloud computing platform, Microsoft has developed the most complete applications, including:

a. Cloud computing service application (Windows Azure, SQL Azure) in the Internet data center.

b. Enterprise online cloud service application (Microsoft Online Services).

c. Enterprise Server (System Center), providing customers the freedom to choose their own solution or mix different solutions.

In order to lead Google, Yahoo! and other existing cloud platforms, Microsoft has also released a self-developed cloud computing platform Azure Services Platform, using the operating system Windows Azure.

5.4. Apple cloud platform

The Apple cloud platform is slightly different from the previous three platforms. When used by users, they must be downloaded to the local user device before being turned on.

Apple's approach is not to treat the cloud as a platform to solve all issues. Instead, the cloud is viewed as a central monitoring station to monitor the user's operation. The main reasons why Apple handles cloud services in this way are as follows:

a. Apple does not trust the quality of current network data delivery, especially the streaming quality provided by mobile phone carriers.

b. Apple does not participate in other systems to share their achievements, as far as possible limited to consumers using Apple devices only to use this service.

c. Apple to reduce replay functionality load, allowing users to play through the cloud, but also if necessary Device download, replay at any time.

Apple cloud platform operating system to cloud data flow rather than control the organization of information transfer. Apple cloud platform operating system applications, music, media, files, messages, photos, backups, settings and other centralized storage in the cloud. iCloud supports all iOS devices. When Apple users use this system to upload files, iCloud automatically backs up the purchased music, applications, files, photos and system devices to other cloud devices and synchronizes them to other Apple devices.

6. Cloud computing security

According to the Cloud Security Alliance (CSA), cloud computing services may encounter seven major information security issues:

1. Unscrupulous people using cloud computing technology to engage in unscrupulous resource services.

2. User operations Interface and cloud computing services with information security concerns.

3. Insiders interested parties, the use of illegal ways to get the cloud client's resource content.
4. Cloud data sharing may cause resource sharing error or interference situation.
5. When the data are all concentrated in the cloud resources platform, may lead to data leakage problems.
6. Cloud client account and password authentication information was intentional tampering.

Information security threats, in addition to man-made attacks, include information system attacks and internal staff operations. There are three steps in protection measures that must be paid special attention to:

1. To strengthen the security protection and setting of hardware and software.
2. Enhance the information system security monitoring and internal operation auditing mechanism.
3. Timely adjustment of information system settings and data backup.

After the cloud computing was put forward, the network attacker also continued to devote himself to attacking the virtual machine. For the self-protection of cloud computing, the following information security recommendations were made:

1. Do not trust the network is a guarantee always safe and secure.
2. Login information on the Internet too detailed, easy to leak personal privacy issues.
3. Whether the data will affect the normal work affairs when the data is placed on the cloud platform.

7. Cloud system virtual technology and pivotal technology

In the cloud system, the most basic software technology is "Virtual Machine" technology. Virtual Machine, or VM for short, is to simulate the host operating system. In recent years, VM technology has been gradually used to simulate different operating systems to support various host needs of cloud users. This is not only the Platform as a Service, the operating system virtualization into network services) core essence of technology. For example, we can host different versions of the Linux operating system, FreeBSD operating system and MS-Windows operating system in the cloud system. The cloud system users can be based on their needs, were connected to the cloud host MS-SQL database services or MySQL database services. For cloud system maintainers, only one cloud host needs to be maintained. However, cloud users do not need to care about the real operating system that the cloud host executes, as long as they can access the data services they need. In this way, the cloud-based SaaS can be completed and the application functions can be virtualized into network services the core technology.

Cloud server virtual host can be roughly divided into two types of server host and client host, server host which is the real hardware computer operating system to host the implementation of the virtual host operating system; and the client host is virtual out of the host system. As long as the hardware capacity permits (memory capacity and hard disk capacity), each server host can execute many different client hosts, each Guest can represent a host, and has an independent IP address and different network Road service. Of course, a more complex cloud architecture can be used as the host of the Guest host, and then host the implementation of different versions of the virtual host operating system, and thus form a "virtual host inside the virtual host." Similar to the nested virtual host architecture (Nest Virtual Machine).

7.1. Pivotal technology—Google File System (GFS)

Google File System (GFS), mainly to deal with the rapid increase in cloud computing data. GFS has all the features of a distributed file system, including storage efficiency, scalability, reliability and reusability, large GFS distributed file system can be composed of hundreds of hard drives, without the use of high-end expensive Storage equipment can maintain the file storage quality. And with fault-tolerant capabilities, GFS easily recovers corrupted files through fault-tolerant detection and auto-recovery in GFS, even in the event of an operation.

When the GFS client client application requests a GFS host server to create a file request, the GFS host server will cut the request into blocks of 64 MB in size, which are then allocated to the lower layer for processing. The file system in order to ensure the safety of the file will automatically copy the block data to at least three backup actions and save them to the hard disk in the ext2 format. Finally, the result of the reassembly process is delivered to the GFS client application, which is the GFS operational flow [1]. As shown in **Figure 1**.

GFS operation process, GFS is mainly used to store metadata, the main namespace file, the partition namespace partition and each file is mapped to the block record location, usually about 64 MB in size, the average of each file only 100 characters, and the real data is stored on the server. In this way, you do not need to worry about the risk of inconsistent backup data of the three lower copies if the server is damaged in an unexpected way, and administrators can also make backups via the remote mechanism so as to be more secure.

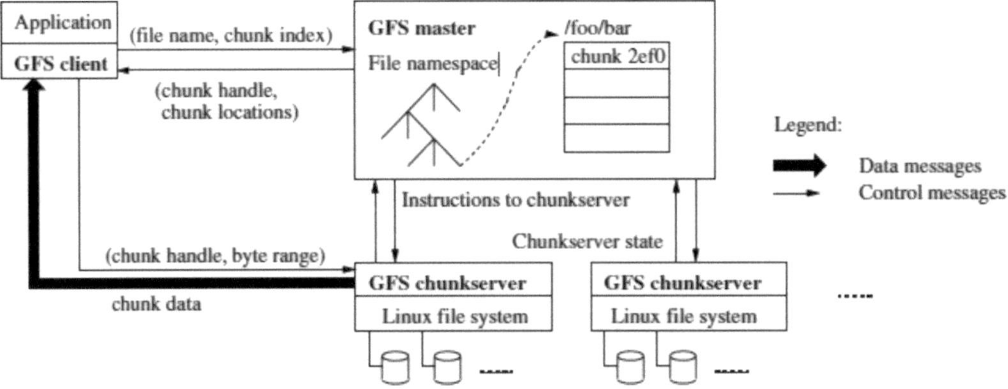

Figure 1. Google File System (GFS) [1].

In addition, 64 MB huge block space has several advantages. First, he reduces the need for communication between the client and the server because the same block space can be processed with only one read for immediate information, and the block storage design can reduce the workload of the search service. Second, because the block space is large, the client usually only needs to operate multiple times in the same block space, which can reduce the number of server switches and reduce the load of network traffic. Third, large block storage space can also reduce the amount of metadata that the main server needs to store. Because of the reduced processing load, you can speed up the main server's connection by placing frequently read metadata on the main server's memory instead of on the hard disk.

7.2. MapReduce

MapReduce is actually a simple programming model. As long as the map and reduce functions are used in programming, the information system helps map to sort out the available data from the original data and classify the available data, and then use the reduce program to simplify the usable data.

The purpose of MapReduce is to run large-scale computer data and the implementation of decentralized computing, for a large number of data to do parallel computing. So the whole structure of MapReduce is composed of two functions Map and Reduce. When the program inputs a large group of key or value, the Map function will automatically disassemble the key or value of many groups, and then Reduce Function simplifies the data content and then merges with the same Key value of the pairing, and finally produce the analysis of the data results [2]. As shown in **Figure 2**.

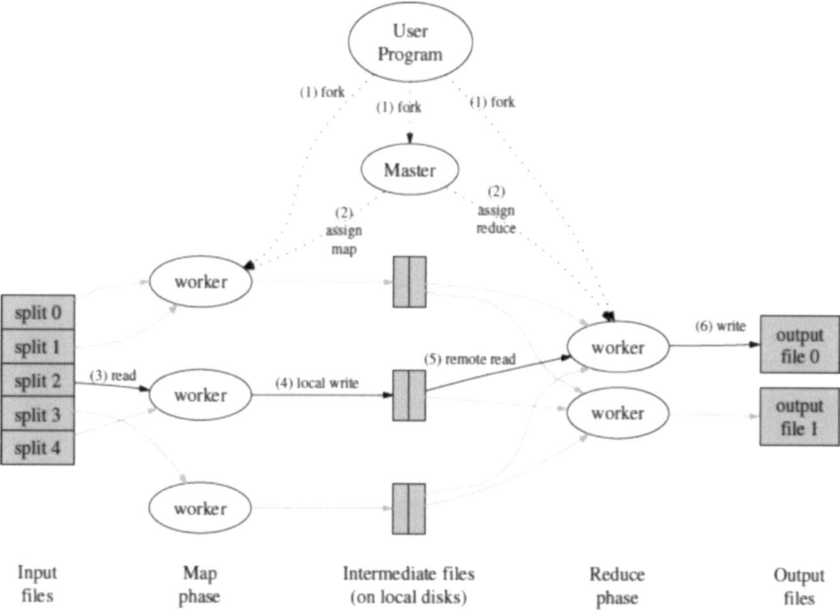

Figure 2. MapReduce [2].

7.3. BigTable

BigTable distributed database query data used in the language of Google Query Language, is a database similar to the SQL command language. Because BigTable can perform complicated analysis and query functions with MapReduce technology architecture, it is especially suitable for integrated data table access up to 10 TB or more.

BigTable storage for the column-oriented, and the traditional relational database row-oriented way, the benefits of the use of column-oriented is very convenient in the new data, each data can be stored in a fixed field of objects. In addition BigTable index of information is divided into two kinds of row key and column key, and can be any string, so more than the traditional relevance of the database with high compression ratio, high read performance.

BigTable the first field is the Row key, the second field is the Column key, the third field is the timestamp as a data index, the three parameters corresponding to the data is stored as a string .

Each basic unit of storage stored in a bigTable has Timstamp, which allows multiple versions of the same stored data over time. And users of the cloud application can specify which data to keep. Since the data type of the timestamp is int64, each storage unit can use the difference of one millionth of a second for storing, so as to completely prevent data from being overwritten [3]. As shown in **Figure 3**.

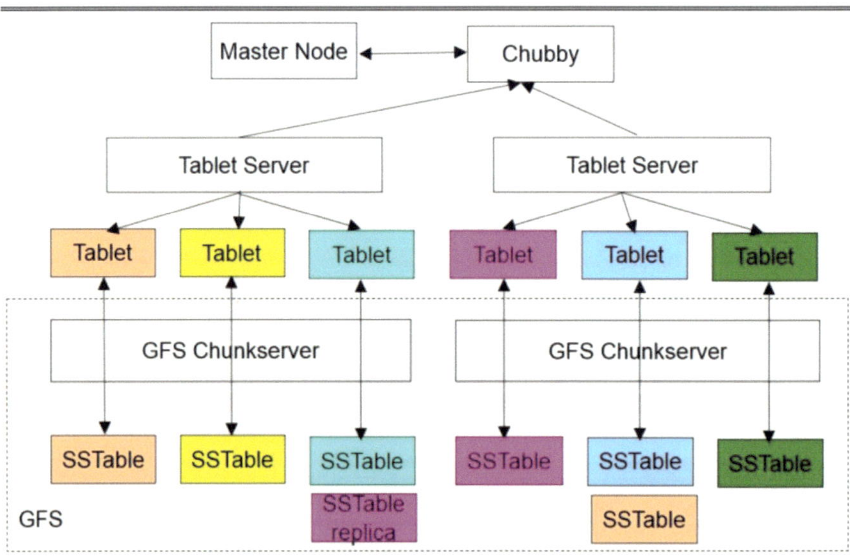

Figure 3. BigTable [3].

8. Case examples

This case example uses PaaS architecture to collect customer consumption data and to analyze the interactions of purchased goods. This study aims to construct a cloud service customized product selection information system to provide a reference to the industry.

The customized products framework of the system is shown in **Figure 4**, in which the relational database management system is used to conduct the data mining which consists of three steps:

The Customized products cloud Information System is shown in **Figure 4**, where the relational database management system is used for data mining that consists of four steps:

Step 1: input the system code by certification and open the databases, which consist of the customer database, the retail mall database, and the transaction database.

Step 2: analyze the data according to the database.

Step 3: transfer the Marketing Knowledge Database to the relevant branches and to the customers.

8.1. Association rule mining

The association rules are proposed by Agrawal and Srikant [5]. Association rule mining is widely used for analyzing the product items purchased by consumers. It is also used to support sales promotion and marketing segmentation. The association rule is represented by X→Y where X and Y are a set of items. This rule means that the transaction records in a business database that contain X tend to contain Y. A large number of valid algorithms for mining association rules have been proposed [7].

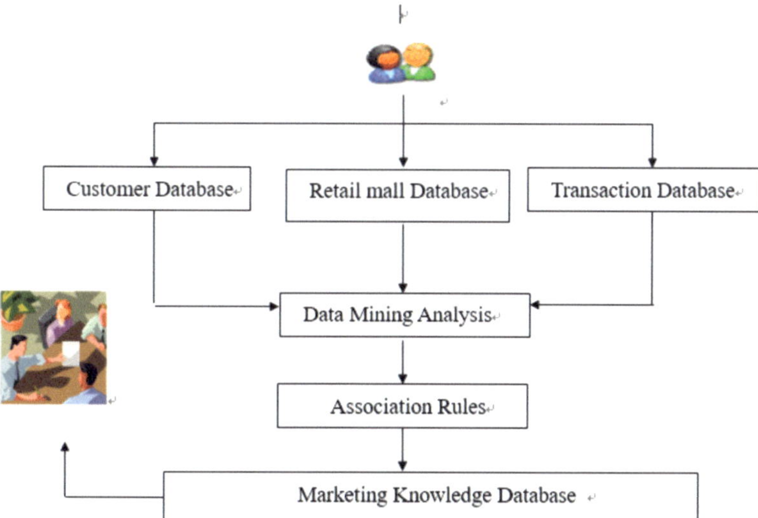

Figure 4. The customized products customized products cloud information system.

In this study, a mining system to detect customer behavior is proposed. The association rules from relational database design are utilized to mine consumer behavior.

In the consumer purchase of computers and memory, for example, the association rules are as follows:

Computer → Memory [support = 25%, confidence = 75%].

The formula shows that 25% of the entire transaction database will buy a computer and memory, while 75% of the total customers who purchase computers will buy them together with memory. The following steps are used to determine the association rules:

1. First, find a collection of high-frequency items (large item set). This collection of support must be greater than the user customized minimum support (minimum support).
2. Second, use a collection of items produced by high-frequency generating association rules.

Currently, many algorithms can identify the high-frequency items associated with a collection of rules, such as Apriori [6] and DHP [8]. Apriori is the most commonly used and best-known algorithm; therefore, its data analysis will be used in this study.

8.2. Customized products analysis

From our interviews with the company marketing managers, the customized products design is the fundamental promotional tool for the firm. The customized products is designed by the marketing office based on decisions from department meetings. For example, more customized products is dedicated to facial care products and decorations products.

The customized products is designed and produced by the marketing office based on aggregated information from head office. The data was collected from June 2015 to May 2016. The database of the system consists of three major parts, namely, customer data, product data, and transaction data.

In this chapter, we propose a cloud service information system prototype using data mining techniques to help enterprises find suitable promotional products for each customer in the cloud customer database.

Step 1: create a basic cloud customer database.

The main characteristic attribute in the collection of user data. It records all possible influence factors of the customer buying behavior attribute data. The cloud customer database is composed of two parts, namely, basic information and preference category. A1 to Ai-1 are the basic properties of the cloud customer information, such as gender, education, salary, and others. Ai records the user's preferences for product categories, such as facial cleanser, Shampoo, and so on.

Step 2: cloud pre-processing of customer databases and program code conversion.

This step is mainly for the retrieval of the required fields from the cloud customer database. Then, the cloud customer attribute data are matched with the users to do the coding to attribute on the clustering.

Step 3: association rules.

http://dx.doi.org/10.5772/intechopen.77283

The first level of association rules uses the product department as decision variables, For example, we let pc, fc, hc, sb, denote the Personal cleaning products department, the Facial care products department, the Home cleaning products department and the Snack biscuits products department, respectively. The equation $P_P(pc \cap fc = Type1 \mid T)$ denotes the probability that the customers will buy products from the Personal cleaning products department and Facial care products department; where type1 and T denote the product combination type1 and customer, respectively. The detailed results are shown in **Table 1**.

The decision variable in the second level association rules is product brand. Herein, three product brands are sold by the Facial care products department (i.e., NIVEA Facial cleanser coded by fc3, Biore Facial cleanser coded by fc1, and Deep Clean Facial cleanser coded by fc2), first product brand is sold by the Home cleaning products department (i.e., Tide Laundry detergent coded by hc2) and second product brands are sold by the Personal cleaning products department (i.e., Biore Body Wash coded by pc2). The equation $P(pc2 \cap fc3 = Type1)$ denotes the probability that the customers will buy pc2 and fc3 simultaneously. Please see **Tables 2** and **3** for more detailed results.

8.3. Marketing knowledge database

According to the mining results, the promotion projects are to design some special customer catalogs for the customer in accordance with the customer's preference for the product brand to enhance product sales.

Product classification as decision variable (step 1)		
Product combination code	Product combination (%)	rank
$pc \cap fc$	56.2	1
$pc \cap hc$	38.6	2
$fc \cap sb$	25.8	3
$fc \cap hc$	16.5	4
$hc \cap sb$	9.8	5

Table 1. Results of section classification as the decision variable (first level).

Product brand as decision variable (step 2)		
Product combination code	Product combination (%)	rank
$pc1 \cap fc3$	82.1	1
$pc2 \cap hc1$	71.5	2
$fc2 \cap sb5$	62.8	3
$fc2 \cap hc3$	53.6	4
$hc6 \cap sb2$	46.3	5

Table 2. Results of product brand (second level).

Decision variable	Combined name of products	Rank
Personal cleaning products department And Facial care products department	a Biore Body Wash paired with a Biore Facial cleanser (85.6%)	1
Personal cleaning products department And Home cleaning products department	a Biore Body Wash paired with a Tide Laundry detergent (72.6%)	2

Table 3. Results of product brand combine (third level).

Figure 5. (Biore Body Wash with and Biore Facial cleanser).

Herein, the special customer promotional products are designed following special customer promotional products 1 and 2 and 3 (SCPP 1 and 2 and 3).

SCPP 1: combine the sale, offering a 15% discount to all customers, of Biore Body Wash with and Biore Facial cleanser, which rank No. 1 in product sales of **Tables 2** and **3** respectively. **Figure 5** shows the description in the special customer promotional products 1.

SCPP 2: combine the sale of Biore Body Wash and tide laundry detergent, which rank No. 2 in product sales of **Tables 2** and **3** respectively, offering a 20% discount to all customers. **Figure 6** shows the description in the special customer promotional products 2.

SCPP 3: combine the sale of Biore Body Wash with the own brand products, offering a 25% discount to all customers. **Figure 7** shows the description in the special customer promotional products 3.

http://dx.doi.org/10.5772/intechopen.77283

Figure 6. (Biore Body Wash and tide laundry detergent).

Figure 7. (Biore Body Wash with the own brand products).

Therefore, when these three indicators by policy makers are found, the needs of individual customer's promotional products shall be considered in the current business situation. The main objective of the promotion is to determine the appropriate weight of each index. The system helps enterprises to efficiently deliver the customized commodity product promotion, as well as really meet the business situation and needs.

9. Conclusion

In this study, association rules were used to identify links between customer profiles and products purchased. It provides marketing managers with a useful tool to rapidly search for valuable information based on customer transaction cloud information, and rapidly establish marketing strategies to enhance sales and profit.

This study provides a cloud service information system that improves the sales of case companies' products by changing the original promotion methods. It can help supervisors and employees to provide them with useful knowledge through the new system presented here to better decide on promotional activities.

After marketing the customized product promotion catalog, the data mining system helps companies understand the market acceptance of the product and understand the product sales, thus repairing its marketing strategy and increasing the sales of the product.

In addition, the data mining system can also amend the design of the customized product catalog based on market sales data and design a customized product catalog for different periods. Therefore, the effective use of data mining systems can help understand the customer's buying behavior, so that decision makers can formulate optimal policies.

Author details

Chien Wen Hung

Address all correspondence to: cwhong@mail.cnu.edu.tw

Department of Information Management, Chia-Nan University of Pharmacy and Science, Tainan, Taiwan

References

[1] Ghemawat S, Gobioff H, Leung S-T. The Google File System. 2003. http://static.googleusercontent.com/external_content/untrusted_dlcp/research.google.com/en/us/archive/gfs-sosp2003.pdf

[2] Dean J, Ghemawat S. MapReduce: Simplified Data Processing on Large Clusters. 2004. https://static.googleusercontent.com/media/research.google.com/zh-TW//archive/mapreduce-osdi04.pdf

[3] Chang F, Dean J, Ghemawat S, Hsieh WC, Wallach DA, Burrows M, Chandra T, Fikes A, Gruber RE. Bigtable: A Distributed Storage System for Structured Data. 2006. https://static.googleusercontent.com/media/research.google.com/zh-TW//archive/bigtable-osdi06.pdf

[4] Elsenpeter RC. Cloud Computing, A Practical Approach. McGraw Hill: Osborne Media; 2009

[5] Agrawal R, Srikant R. Mining sequential pattern. In: Proc. of the 11th International Conference on Data Engineering. Vol. 12. 1995. pp. 3-14

[6] Aaker DA. Measuring brand equity across products and markets. California Management Review. 1996;**38**(3):103-120

[7] Anand SS, Patrick AR, Hughes JG, Bell DA. A data mining methodology for cross-sales. Knowledge-Based Systems. 1998;**10**:449-461

[8] Leonard H, Eduardo LR, Stefan V. A cloud brokerage approach for solving the resource management problem in multi-cloud environments. Computers & Industrial Engineering. 2016;**95**:16-26

Chapter 3

Evaluation Theory for Characteristics of Cloud Identity Trust Framework

Eghbal Ghazizadeh and Brian Cusack

Additional information is available at the end of the chapter

http://dx.doi.org/10.5772/intechopen.76338

Abstract

Trust management is a prominent area of security in cloud computing because insufficient trust management hinders cloud growth. Trust management systems can help cloud users to make the best decision regarding the security, privacy, Quality of Protection (QoP), and Quality of Service (QoS). A Trust model acts as a security strength evaluator and ranking service for the cloud and cloud identity applications and services. It might be used as a benchmark to setup the cloud identity service security and to find the inadequacies and enhancements in cloud infrastructure. This chapter addresses the concerns of evaluating cloud trust management systems, data gathering, and synthesis of theory and data. The conclusion is that the relationship between cloud identity providers and Cloud identity users can greatly benefit from the evaluation and critical review of current trust models.

Keywords: cloud computing, cloud security, federated identity management system, cloud identity, trust frameworks

1. Introduction

Trust management had been established by Blaze, Feigenbaum and Lacy [1] to deal with security issues of centralized systems. The aim of their system was overcoming the inflexibility of a complex trust relationship, and centralized control of trust relationship. Trust management has been attractive by many researchers especially in the area of Peer to Peer, E-Commerce, Wireless Sensor Network, Grid Computing, and Cloud Computing [2]. There are several trust definitions but in this book chapter trust means the extent to which Cloud Identity users (CIdU) and Cloud Service Providers (CSP) are willing to depend on a CIdPs and Cloud Service

Customers (CSC) provisioning and de-provisioning their service and expect certain qualities that CIdPs promised to be met.

In the cloud computing, user and provider recommendation has been adopted as a trust [3]. The reason for widely using is to get the advantage of user and provider about the Trust Service Provider (TSP). Though, in the social psychology, it is well-known that the role of a service customer has a substantial influence on another customers' trust assessment. However, transitive recommendation and explicit recommendation are different forms of recommendation. Therefore, in the explicit recommendation, a consumer of the cloud clearly recommend a particular TSP, but, in the transitive recommendation, on the other hand, a cloud customer trusts a particular TSP because at least one of her trusted relations trusts the service. The reputation of the TSP is consequently related to the customer's feedback of TSP which highlight the importance of the trust. [5]. Moreover, as pointed in [6] reputation can have a direct or indirect influence on the trustworthiness of a TSP and CSP. Nevertheless, Unlike the recommendation, in reputation, cloud service consumers do not know the source of the trust feedback, because there are no trusted relations in reputation systems. eBay, Amazon, Aliexpress, and Epinions are some examples of online reputation-based systems and review systems where the consumer's opinions and reviews on specific products or services are expressed.

Therefore, the complexity and variety of the trust in the cloud area is one contemporary issue in which the research community has recently embarked. Manifesting itself as the descendant of several other trust framework such as user observation and computational frameworks inherits their limitations and advancements. Towards the end-goal of a thorough comprehension of the field of cloud identity trust framework, and a more rapid adoption from the scientific community, we propose in this chapter an ontology of trust framework which demonstrates a dissection of the trust frameworks into six main frameworks based on their characteristics and methods of data collection to help and improve user's knowledge based decision making. Moreover, evaluation theory leads this chapter to illustrates their interrelations as well as their inter-dependency on trust elements and attributes. The contribution of this chapter lies in being one of the first research and attempts to establish a dedicated ontology and taxonomy of the cloud identity trust framework with regards of the evaluation theory. Therefore, Better comprehension of the trust elements would enable and leads the CIdPs to design more trustworthy services and gateways for the CIdUs and facilitate the selection of the identity providers. In turn, this will assist the identity community to accelerate its contributions and insights into this evolving identity field.

2. Evaluation system architecture

Evaluation is a key analytical process in all intellectual, disciplines, and service providers [7]. Also, it is possible to apply different types of evaluation methods to provide knowledge of the complexity and ubiquity of the cloud service providers. This book chapter aim is to obtain a set of basic evaluation components based on the [8]. Moreover, this book chapter aims to propose a framework that can be used to develop a trusted computing with the purpose of improving the previous trust methods. In particular, evaluation system architecture method had been applied to review the trust establishment frameworks by means of the identification of the evaluation components and the analysis of their weaknesses and strengths. Therefore, this

http://dx.doi.org/10.5772/intechopen.76338

book chapter seeks to highlight that related work of mentioned trust framework developed based on trust theoretical and practical foundation. In this section, evaluation theory [8] is considered as a theoretical foundation for developing cloud identity trust framework and its processes has been shown in **Figure 1**.

Comprehensive and reliable of the trust level evaluation in identity environment are two crucial reasons to use evaluation theory. Evaluation theory offers a formal and clear description of the concept of evaluation. Therefore, it proposes six components involved in an evaluation shown in **Figure 2** and will be adopted and discussed in the following sub-sections.

- Target: Trust between CIdPs and CIdUs
- Criteria: Trust elements of the Cloud Identity Providers (CIdP) and CSPs that are to be evaluated
- Yardstick or standard: the ideal trust framework against which the current trust framework is to be compared
- Data-gathering techniques: Critical or systematic literature review needed to obtain data to analyze each criterion
- Synthesis techniques: Generally this technique used to judge the target, obtaining the results of the evaluation with judging each particular element,
- Evaluation process: series of activities and tasks by means of which an evaluation is performed (out of scope for this book chapter)

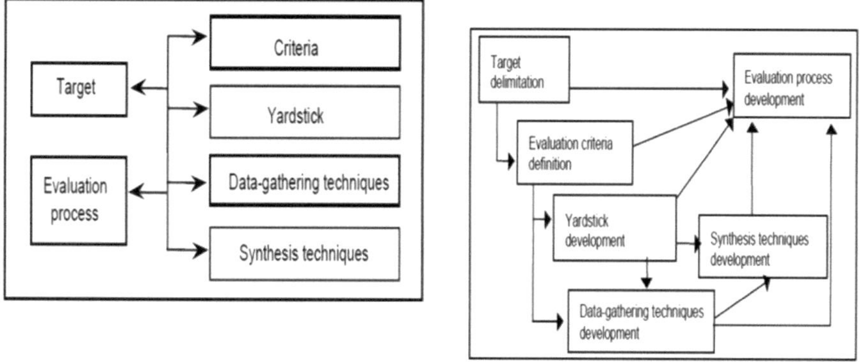

Figure 1. Components of an evaluation and their interrelations ([8], p. 6).

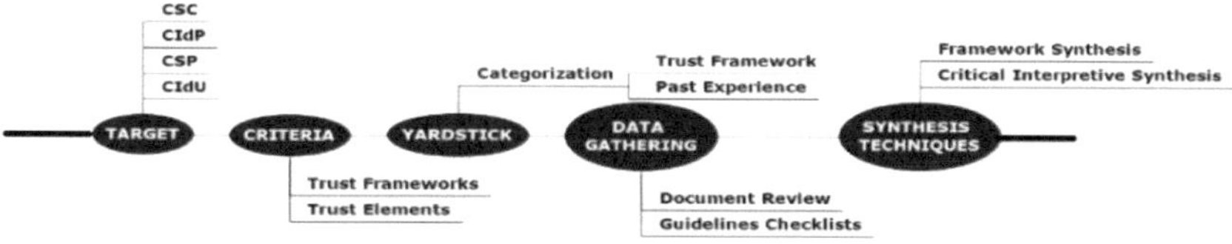

Figure 2. Cloud identity trust evaluation framework.

2.1. Target

The first activity as shown in **Figure 2** is identifying and ascertaining evaluation target. A target which means the object under evaluation provides knowledge about what the object is and presents a general description of the objective functions and domains. Therefore, in this book chapter level of trust for CIdPs has been selected to be the object under evaluation. It has been chosen because CSPs have not yet adopted an all-out cloud identity and they require identity federation in order to provide not only SSO but also agile and secure access controls between internal and external services. Besides, to enable communications among CIdPs, CIdUs, CSPs, they must be able to establish trust with one another and exchange identity information. Therefore, cloud identity trust framework has been developed to help CIdUs make a good decision based on the trust elements.

2.2. Evaluation criteria

Criteria definition is the second critical and essential step in developing a cloud identity trust framework. Having ascertained and delimited the target (CIdP), it is necessary to identify what characteristics (trust elements) of the target (CIdP) are important for evaluation purposes. These characteristics are referred to as evaluation criteria. Alabool and Mahmood [7] specified the importance to use as many criteria as possible to make better trust elements coverage under evaluation. These criteria also can pertain to diverse Sub-elements; while each sub-elements also can be broken down several elements. A critical literature review (overview of published materials) study has been conducted to answer two questions.

First, what is the current state of trust computing knowledge about these issues and problems (Looking for the taxonomy and methods of trust framework as shown in **Figure 2**)?

Second, what are the current trust computing in the theoretical or policy issues and debates related to trust, cloud computing, and cloud identity management systems (Looking for elements and cloud identity trust elements as shown in **Figure 2**)?

To answer the first question, there was a need for caching module to effectively communicate with CSCs. Attributes of a CSPs are used as evidence to make trust judgment on their service, and those attributes need to be distributed in a trustworthy way. In the following, attribute certification as an approach to deliver cloud attributes will be discussed. Hence, it had motivated to build a hybrid model for trust management in cloud identity computing environments. Current trends and existing approaches in the field of trust establishment need to be categorized in a precise way to identify and analyze the current cloud trust establishment method. In this regard, user observation, Auditing and Risk Assessment, Self-assessment Questionnaires, Benchmarking and Monitoring, Service Level Agreement (SLA) Based Trust framework, and Computational Trust Framework have been systematically categorized as a proposed trust models on the basis of their diverse attributes and techniques for calculating the trust score as a source of evidences and **Figure 3** shows the selected categories for this book chapter.

User observation: Users opinion, social network, and reputation based approaches are some of the user observation frameworks. The reputation of CSP is the aggregated opinion of CSCs

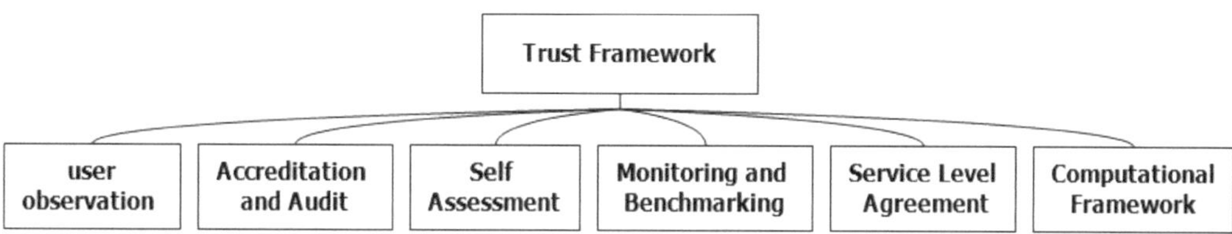

Figure 3. Taxonomy of trust frameworks.

towards that provider and the services whereas trust is between two entities. Usually, the high reputation indicates the high trust and customers who need to make trust judgment on a provider, may use the reputation to calculate or estimate the trust level of that provider. The result is a comprehensive score reflecting the overall opinion of the CSCs or a small number of scores on several major aspects of performance [9]. The social network based approach is an analog of how a person initially trusts an entity, unknown before in the real world. Moreover, when a cloud user has only limited direct experience with a cloud service, other users' opinions could be an important source of cloud attribute assessment.

Self-assessment: It is a free publicly accessible registry which allows CSPs and CIdPs to publish self-assessment of their security controls, in either a questionnaire or a matrix. It shows and determines how CIdPs and CSPs align with the security guidelines. However, the information offered is a cloud provider's self -assessment; cloud users may want assessments performed by some independent third-party professional organizations like CSA stare two and three [10].

Accreditation and audit: Generally, the trust elements and characteristics of CSPs need to be verified before use for decision CSCs' decision making. Therefore, it is expected assertions from third-party independent professional organizations. Trust solution provides cloud users a solution where the overall processes of cloud trust management can be delegated to third-party professionals. Though, similarly, the basis for cloud users to trust them needs to be established. Therefore, one possible solution is formal accreditation and audit to the trust mechanism problems. Auditing and risk assessment will be considered in this book chapter as a category of trust establishment and independent authority in the identity area. External audits, attestations, or certifications for the more general purpose have been used in practice.

Monitoring and benchmarking: It is needed to continuously measure and assess infrastructure or application behavior for performance, reliability, power usage, ability to meet SLAs and security to perform business analytics, for improving the operation of systems and applications, and for several other activities.

Service level agreement: In practice, one way to establish a trust for cloud providers is the fulfillment of SLAs. SLA validation and monitoring schemes are used to quantify what exactly a cloud provider is offering and which assurances are actually met [11]. Numerous works have been carried out to define SLA metrics in cloud computing. The SLA metrics selected in this study assess the cloud services from appropriate cloud providers and help this research to find the SLA gaps.

Computational framework: It is focusing on mathematically formal frameworks for measuring the level of trust, including modeling, languages, and algorithms for computing trust. It is integrated method of previous methods and new methods to eliminate trust elements, prioritize, formulate and disseminate level of providers' trust [12].

To answer for the second question, in this analysis step, this research seeks to draw upon key findings from related work on cloud computing, federated identity management, and trust computing, which aim to extend these trust elements through identifying characteristics and attributes of cloud and cloud identity providers. To do so, in this book chapter question number two has been split into two questions and struggles to answer these two questions which have been mention before.

Between cloud provider and cloud consumer, what are the Essential System Attributes (ESA) of trust establishment?

Between CldPs and CldUs, what are the Essential System Characteristics (ESC) of published trust establishment method?

Figure 4 illustrates the components of common trust framework which is based on the [13]. Based on this figure, as shown, indirect information like recommendations and direct observations are valuable for the any TSPs, CldP, and CSPs. Moreover, the trust level is dynamic based on the provider interaction. Therefore, the trust level is based on the different factors such as but not limited monitoring, trust background and history, qualitative, and quantitative elements.

Therefore, the cloud customers will have the ability to select the services based on the ranking, real-time performance and. However, the key elements for the common trust frameworks based on the literature and previous research are:

Figure 4. Service trust evaluation system architecture.

http://dx.doi.org/10.5772/intechopen.76338

Cloud entities: This part responsible for communication with cloud customers and understanding their level of trust and application, and search and ranking of suitable trusted services using other components such as but not limited the direct or indirect trust, evaluation method, and trust management.

Monitoring and history information: this part searches for providers that can provide customers' requirements. Therefore, the direct and indirect trust will be monitoring during the time of service providing. In the meanwhile, these results will be saved in the trust level's database of the specific provider.

Computing service network structure and catalog: One of the main feature of cloud is transparency, which help the CSPs to advertise their features. Therefore, measurement of various service trust evaluation and the trust evaluation of service providers are two issues which arise based on this research and previous researches [12, 14, 15] which will be identified in this book chapter. A set of dimensions to study trust management issues where each layer of the framework has several dimensions have been identified in this section. These dimensions are identified by considering the highly dynamic, distributed, and non-transparent nature of cloud environments. Therefore, in this book chapter the dimension for the evaluation has been categorized in three separate areas which will be explained in the rest of this section.

2.2.1. *Cloud entities*

Cloud brokers, cloud resellers, cloud consumers, and cloud auditors are four primary entities in the cloud evaluation environment [16]. They each playing a different role and were identified by NIST [17]. However, in this sub-section, five cloud entities' trust evaluation issues will be explained and their trust relationship will be identified.

Credibility: It refers to the quality of the information or service that makes cloud entities trust the information or service [18, 19]. The credibility evaluation appears in several forms including the entity's credibility and the feedback credibility. For instance, lack of proper identity scheme, will cause easily leads to low accuracy of the trust level because trust management system suffers attacks such as Sybil attacks [20].

Privacy: The transparency feature of the CSPs and interactions with the Service Measurement Index (SMI), or Cloud Security Alliance Security, Trust & Assurance Registry (CSA STAR) suffers the privacy of the providers because it discloses the sensitive information of the entities. Indeed, cryptographic encryption techniques is essential when these providers interact with trust system management, but, the point is these techniques are inadequate in cloud environments due to its highly dynamic and distributed nature [21].

Personalization: It refers to the degree of autonomy in which the cloud entities adhere to the trust management rules. Both can have proper personalization in their feedback designs and executions. This means that cloud entities can select the trust process and the techniques they prefer. Personalization is applicable if the trust management system has fully autonomous collaboration, where each participant needs to interact via well-defined interfaces that allow participants to have control over their trust level and the flexibility to change their trust processes without affecting each other. It is difficult to have a fully autonomous collaboration because of the complex translation features it requires [22].

Integration: It refers to the ability to integrate different trust management perspectives and techniques. Entities can give their security elements from different perspectives through different trust management techniques. Combining several trust management techniques can generally increase the accuracy of the trust results [23].

Security: It refers to the degree of dissemination protection that the entities and trust assessments has against malicious behaviors and attacks. The Cloud Trust Protocol (CTP) [24] is the mechanism by which some of the cloud entities ask for and receive information about the elements of transparency as applied to cloud service providers. The primary purpose of the CTP and the elements of transparency is to generate evidence-based confidence that everything that is claimed to be happening in the cloud is indeed happening as described.

2.2.2. Computing

A trust evaluation system should be able to evaluate and compute the trust relationships between CSPs and CSCs, which will significantly affect the level of trust. On the other hand, identifying trust computing methods and their perspectives, techniques, adaptability, security, and scalability are remained an important challenging issues in the trust management area [14, 25]. Therefore, in this sub-section the importance of these issues will be explained.

Perspective: Some trust management approaches focus on the CSP's perspective while others focus on the CSC's perspective. It is therefore crucial to determine the perspective supported by a trust assessment function. The more perspectives the trust management system supports, the more comprehensive the trust management system becomes [26].

Technique: It refers to the degree to which a technique can be adopted by the trust management system to manage and assess trust attributes. It is important to differentiate between the trust assessments functions that adopts a certain technique for trust management from the ones that adopt several trust management techniques together. Adopting several trust management techniques together can increase the accuracy of the trust results [9].

Adaptability: It refers to how quickly the trust assessment function can adapt to changes of the inquisitive cloud entities. Some trust assessment inquiries can follow certain customized criteria from the inquisitive parties (e.g., weighing the elements based on the user's expectation), while others may follow the general trust assessment metric. In addition, updating trust results may be used as another indicator of adaptability because of the highly dynamic nature of cloud environments where new cloud service providers and consumers can join while others might leave at any time [27].

Security: It refers to the degree of robustness of the trust assessment function against malicious behaviors and attacks. The computing function security level and the communication security level are two different security levels where attacks can occur. In the computing layer, there are several potential attacks against the trust assessment function including whitewashing, self-promoting, and slandering [28]. At the communication security level, there are several attacks such as Man-in-the-Middle (MITM) attack and Denial-of-Service (DoS) attack or distributed Denial-of-Service (DDoS) attack [29].

Scalability: It is important that the cloud computing trust management system be scalable because it is highly dynamic and distributed nature of cloud environments. It refers to the ability of the trust computing system to grow in one or more characteristics. Trust models that follow a centralized architecture are more prone to several problems including scalability, availability, and security [30].

2.2.3. *Monitoring and history*

A trust evaluation system should be able to measure the truthfulness of entities based on the qualitative, quantitative, Semi-qualitative, entities' history, and monitoring methods [3, 14, 15, 18, 27]. Hence, a reliable trust management system depends on the response time, redundancy, and accuracy and capability of collecting and filtering the trust essential attributes and characteristics.

Response time: Lack of fast responding or delay to handle trust assessment inquiries by the trust framework leads inaccuracy of the distribute trust results, particularly when there is a significant number of CSPs and CSCs [31, 32].

Redundancy: As redundancy is one of the main attributes of cloud, consequently, the degree of the trust management redundancy is crucial to manage and assess the trust feedback. There are two redundancy approaches in cloud environment: First, assessment redundancy which occurs when multiple trust assessment inquiries are issued sequentially for the same cloud service. Second, data redundancy used to avoid scalability and monitoring issues. Redundancy causes resource waste and eventually affects the performance of the trust management system [33].

Accuracy: it refers to the degree of correctness of the monitoring, history, quantitative or qualitative results that can be determined through one or more accuracy attributes such as the unique identification of trust characteristics and using the proper techniques to disseminate the trust level. Poor identification of characteristics can lead to inaccurate trust results [9].

2.3. Evaluation yardstick

A yardstick can be defined as the ideal target which is trust identity management against which the real target is to compare. Yardstick [8] is a measure of standard used for comparison or to judge a certain target. For example, grouping evaluation criteria and then compare these criteria one by one with the yardstick is one of the most well-known approaches. In this study, criteria are categorized and evaluated depending on cloud trust framework and past experiences and knowledge.

2.3.1. *Trust framework and past experience*

Lack of the proper information and past experience of the CSPs leads the weak decision by the CSCs. Hence, many researchers [3, 27, 34–36] have conducted a research to compare and evaluate the level of the services that user gain by the CSPs. For example, in a typical distributed environment [37], an agent (trustier) is acting in a domain where he needs to trust other agents or objects, whose ability and reliability are unknown. The trustier agent queries the trust system to gather more knowledge about the trustee agent and better ground its decision. However, a trust-based decision in a specific domain is a multi-stage process. But, the first step is the identification and selection of the appropriate input data. These data are in general, domain-specific, and identified through an analysis conducted over the application.

2.4. Data gathering techniques

"You can't control what you can't measure ([38], p. 1)". Measurement, assignation, and opinion are three main data-gathering techniques used in most evaluations in the IT environment. They are required to obtain data to analyze each evaluation criterion [8]. Measurement involves the use of the appropriate documents and guidelines to extract the criteria. For the assignation, documentation inspection has been assigned. Besides, observation techniques for getting subjective criteria data has been applied for opinion step. The primary goal of this part is to provide decision makers (CIdUs and CSCs) with information as complete as possible. In this book chapter, document review and numerous guidelines such as National Checklist Program for IT Products [39], Union Agency for Network and Information Security (ENISA) Auditing Framework for Trust Service Providers [40], and National Institute of Standards and Technology (NIST) Guidelines for Access Control System Evaluation Metrics [41] are the main data gathering techniques that used to collect data and information regard each criteria. Document reviews method of gathering data by reviewing documents that provide information about the characteristics, design, guidelines, requirements, and implementation process related to CIdPs and their responsibilities. While checklist refers to a series of commands and instructions for verifying that the product has been operated correctly [39]. This study used the proposed categorized frameworks as shown in **Figure 2** and proposed ESA which explained in general in 2.2 and will be explained in detail in the next part. The first trust elements (ESA) are developed to identify the essential cloud computing attributes according to cloud security, privacy, and trust attributes. The second trust elements (ESC) is designed to identify the essential cloud identity providers' characteristics regarding trust, security, and privacy.

The aim of ESC of Cloud Identity section is to highlight the major security, privacy, and trust issues in current existing cloud identity computing environments. The detailed analysis of the selected studies is based on their similarities in terms of the trust computing, cloud computing, and cloud identity.

2.5. Synthesis technique

Synthesis technique refers to a set of relative activities and stages to synthesize all information and data which are essential for each system criterion and elaborate in order to evaluate CIdP against [8]. In this book chapter, in order to synthesize the information obtained from documents review and guidelines a hybrid evaluation (cloud identity trust evaluation framework (**Figure 2**)) and ranking technique has been developed by integrated critical interpretive [42] and framework technique [43]. Therefore, better comprehension of the trust elements and essential cloud identity provider trust characteristics (2.5.1) would enable the identity management systems to design more efficient system and applications for the CldUs and CSCs and facilitate the adoption of this novel elements in their environments. In turn, this will assist the identity community to promote their contributions and insights into this evolving identity field.

2.5.1. *Essential cloud identity provider trust characteristics*

There can be several identity providers offering cloud-based identity services with similar functionalities (Habiba et al., [4]). CldUs are interested to select identity providers not only based on the functional characteristics but also based on non-functional characteristics. This refers to how well CldP behaves and what sort of capabilities the providers possess regarding non-functional attributes. In Cloud identity environments, according to (Habib et al., 2012) those attributes go beyond the non-functional QoS parameters, which are considered important for selecting trustworthy web service providers.

SLA is a common practice that identity providers consider in order to build a contractual relationship with a potential consumer. In the context of SLA, identity users trust an identity provider to provide compensation in the case of violation of specific clauses in the agreement. Therefore, in this section of research will attempt to identify the ESC of the cloud identity systems. These characteristics would help both CldUs and CldPs understand the importance of these features that are worth considering when selecting or implementing the CIDMS. Moreover, PKI is a widely used mature technology that employs trust mechanisms to support, key certification and validation, digital signature, attribute certification and validation. But the question is can researcher apply trust ideas used in PKI to establish trust mechanisms to the cloud? Huang and Nicol [9] identified and answered this question and mentioned that this raises questions that ask about the foundation of that trust, and how the trust is inferred or calculated. They suggested that the trust comes from recommendations along the chain of certificates by those certificate issuers, but the practice of digital certification and validation in real PKI systems suggests that the trust comes from compliance with certain certificate policies. However, certificate policies play a central role in PKI trust, therefore, PKI will be a policy-based trust.

The main goal of the ESC of CldP is to highlight the major trust, privacy, and security issues in the existing cloud federated identity environments. The method and technique for this part can be summarized as: surveying the major trust, privacy, and security issues that lead threats in the existing cloud federated identity environments; and evaluating the methods which be addressed to minimize this potential trust, privacy, and security threats, and providing a high level of trust, security, and privacy. So, this section analyses the main attributes, which help in assessing the CldPs operational trust.

2.5.1.1. *Balancing*

As nowadays is the era of data explosion and big data, especially in the cloud environment and indeed the amount of data storage increases quickly, trust framework should be dynamic and align with the latest technology of the balancing. So, load balancing is one of the main challenges which is required to distribute the dynamic workload across multiple nodes to ensure that no single node is overwhelmed. However, by balancing and distributing the load between numerous resources, the performance of the services will be improving. Therefore, CSPs and CIdPs should be flexible, automated, and extensible by involving the latest standards and best practices. Meeting these criteria is essential to ensure the long-term success of a cloud balancing strategy. But, combining high availability with security is arising the importance of the resource and infrastructure management. To sum up, the ability to distribute connections across the globe based on device type, geographic location, the state of servers in one location or another, and balanced loads is essential system characteristics [44].

2.5.1.2. Single sign on

Authentication across multiple vendors is one of the first issues that should be solved in Cloud area. SSO technology, regarding data protection, confidentiality, and privacy issues can be limited by the different barriers. SSO streamlines secure access to all applications and resources with one set of credentials, regardless cloud, mobile, web, and VPN resources. The result is an improved user experience and trust without tedious login procedures and high friction authentication workflows and user-friendly. SSO is a simple solution to user identity issues because since they are already authenticated, no password is required and because no password is required, there is no password for anyone to steal. It increased application adoption, employee productivity, and decreased helpdesk costs [45].

2.5.1.3. Lifecycle

The goal of cloud lifecycle management is to manage the dynamic nature of the cloud environment, accelerating provisioning, facilitating flexibility, and rapidly meeting the needs of the business. With the cloud lifecycle management solution, organizations can deliver flexible, customizable cloud services while maintaining a structured, controlled, and dynamic IT environment. Moreover, Iriberri and Leroy [46] indicated the features that should be selected and gradually added depending on the type of community under development and the purpose of the community as shown in **Figure 5**.

2.5.1.4. Privacy

Identity management systems have existed offering privacy and anonymity in a the cloud environment for CIdUs [47]. Trust management, as well as efficient CIDMS and user keys, are required to achieve privacy. It is therefore difficult to design a system which provides privacy and security to the sensitive CIdUs' data. As a result, there is a significant gap between CIDPs' claim and CIdUs' views of the cloud's privacy and security [48].

2.5.1.5. Risk

Among all privacy and security issues, this part treats the challenges posed by identity management in the cloud, focusing on risk assessment. Federation as a vital feature of cloud and cloud identity needs strong integration, cooperation, and collaboration among different clouds. Consequently, it introduces complex tasks in risk assessment to quantify CIdPs and investigate new metrics in the CIDMS [49]. Djemame, Armstrong, Guitart, and Macias [50] designed a risk assessment model and focused on a specific aspect of risk assessment applied

http://dx.doi.org/10.5772/intechopen.76338

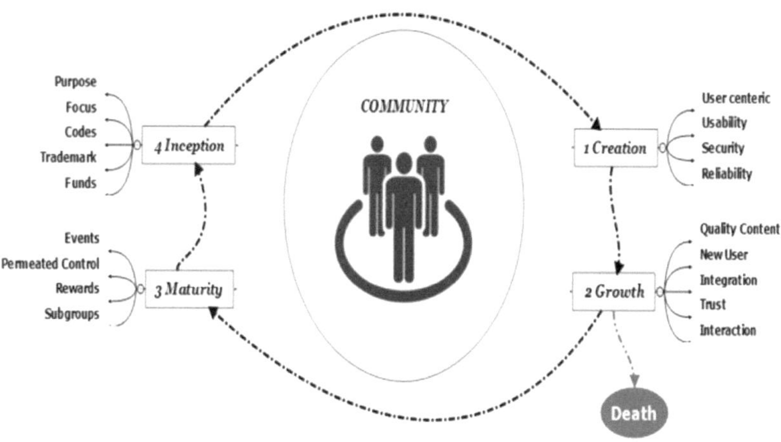

Figure 5. Online community life-cycle perspective ([45], p. 9).

in cloud computing and they described the various stages in the service lifecycle whereas risk assessment takes place. Theoharidou et al. [51] examined privacy risk assessment for cloud and identifies threats, vulnerabilities, and countermeasures that clients and providers should implement in order to achieve privacy compliance and accountability.

2.5.1.6. Standard

Securing information and the systems that store, process, and transmit users' identity information is a challenging task for organizations. Standardized facilitates to collect, verify, and update system security configurations and they can work in concert or be implemented separately. It also would allow authentication to be automated. The goal of any authentication standard is to produce technical specifications that define an open, scalable, interoperable set of mechanisms that reduce the reliance on passwords to authenticate users and to operate industry programs to help ensure successful worldwide adoption of the user authentication.

There are six methods and standards that industry collaborates to make major progress in term of mitigating identity theft and improve strong authentication. The first one continues with Fast IDentity Online (FIDO) [52] to eliminate the password by strong authentication tight with the hardware. There is a need of keep working with fishing protection like Internet Engineering Task Force (IETF) [53] and Organization for the Advancement of Structured Information Standards (OASIS). Work for share intelligence and IP practically OpenID Connect Reduced Instruction Set Computing (OIDC-RISC) is super important for the strong authentication. There are two new methods, token binding and session revocation. The aim of token binding is to mitigate impersonate a user identity by binding token with hardware against man in the middle attack. CIdUs want to revoke all sessions and access tokens that have been handed out.

2.5.1.7. Eliminating password

Fast Identity Online (FIDO) and Wide Web Consortium (W3C) (WebAuthn) could eliminate, or at least significantly mitigate the risk of passwords. The mission of these standards is to define a client-side API that provides strong authentication functionality to Web Applications.

This specification standard helps simplify and improve the security of authentication. As the steward for the Web platform, the W3C is uniquely positioned to focus the attention of Web infrastructure providers and developers on the shortcomings of passwords and the necessity of their replacement. The FIDO protocol employs public key cryptography, relying on users' devices to generate key pairs during a registration process. The user's device retains the generated private key and delivers the public key to the service provider. The service provider retains this key, associates it with a user's account, and when a login request is received, issues a challenge that must be signed by the private key holder as a response [54].

2.5.1.8. Phishing protection

Phishing is a technique that involves user to steal confidential information and passwords by using email. Security Automation and Continuous Monitoring (SACM) reuse existing protocols, mechanisms, information and data models preferably Internet Engineering Task Force (IETF) standards that could support automation of asset, change, configuration, and vulnerability management. Therefore, Trusted Automated Exchange of Indicator Information (TAXII), Cyber Observable Expression (CybOX), and Structured Threat Information Expression (STIX), as some common foundational cybersecurity specifications are now being advanced through the OASIS and they will support sharing for cyber security situational awareness, automated information analysis, real-time network defense, and sophisticated threat characterization and response. Obviously, Security professionals are overwhelmed and simply do not have time for analyzing data in disparate formats. Therefore, TAXII, CybOX, STIX are focusing on cyber intelligence to analyzing data in the cloud. Hence, STIX is a language for describing cyber threat information, TAXII defines services and message exchanges that enable organizations to share the information they choose with the providers they choose, however, CybOX is a language for specifying, capturing, and communicating events properties that are observable in cloud area [55]. To sum up, the ability to analyzing the threat and phishing protection is essential system characteristics for any CSPs, and especially any CIdPs.

2.5.1.9. Shared intelligence and IP

The ability to react quickly to identity theft attacks will effectively stop the access of hackers before they grape CSC's information. But, it requires a trusted community wherein organizations share security and threat intelligence, such as IP addresses of attackers, new types of malware or techniques criminals are engaging. The goal of Risk and Incident Sharing and Coordination (RISC) is to provide privacy recommendations, data sharing schemas, and protocols to Share information about critical events in order to thwart attackers from leveraging compromised accounts from one CSPs to gain access to accounts on other CSPs and enable both CSPs and CSCs to coordinate in order to securely restore accounts following a compromise [56]. Therefore, TAXII, CybOX, and STIX are an open community-driven effort that help with the automated exchange of identity theft information. This allows identity theft information to be represented in a standardized format and it is essential system characteristics for any CIdPs. So, the intelligence combination of STIX and TAXII allow researchers and developers to easily share consistence identity information [57].

2.5.1.10. *Token binding*

CIdPs generate various security tokens such as OAuth tokens for CIdUs to access cloud service providers. Attackers export bearer tokens from CIdU machines or from compromised network connections, present these bearer tokens to CSPs and impersonate authenticated users. Token Binding enables defense against such attacks by cryptographically binding security tokens to a secret held by the CIdU [58].

2.5.1.11. *Session revocation*

In term of any CIdUs' system compromising, they want a way to revoke all sessions and access tokens that have been handed out. It is important that any outstanding access tokens are not revoked by clicking Logout all. They have to expire naturally. Based on the OIDC standard, Revoke refresh token, SSO Session Idle, SSO Session Max, Offline Session Idle, Access Token Lifespan, and client login timeout are some term should be considered in cloud federated identity management systems [59].

2.5.1.12. *Interning of thing*

There are seemingly competing, complex security requirements to be deployed on IoT platform with potentially limited resources like authenticate to multiple networks securely, and provide strong authentication and data protection. Thus IoT must be secure in order for its value to be realized. If we do not have confidence of what IoT entity, then we cannot protect the potentially sensitive sensor data being shared or the transactions being conducted [60].

The Cloud Security Alliance (CSA) has established the IoT Working Group (WG) [61] to focus on providing relevant guidance to cloud users who are implementing IoT solutions. Their aim is to provide understandable recommendations to information technology staff charged with securely implementing and deploying IoT solutions considering IoT Identity and Access Management (IAM). Moreover, ISO 27 is to development of standards for the protection of information and ICT. This includes generic methods, techniques, and guidelines to address both security and privacy aspects such as security aspects of identity management, biometrics and privacy [62].

3. Conclusion

In conclusion, the chapter has provided an evaluation framework for the relationship between cloud service providers and cloud service users. It critically evaluates the context and provides an assessment of the current trust models that are available and suggests that further innovation is required. A justification for the selection of a CIdPs is made and a framework for decision-making provided. In addition, data gathering tools have been provided and guidance on the synthesis of theory and data made. A hybrid MCDM technique is advocated for trust evaluation in fuzzy and complex environments, in order to effectively evaluate and prioritize trust elements. Each element of the research contributes a partial view of cloud trust, and the suggested improvements will lead towards a complete picture of how cloud identity entities work together to form an integrated trust system. It will have a solid grounding in trust, serving to facilitate trusted paths to trusted cloud identity services. Furthermore, these models need to incorporate all aspects of security quantification measures for cloud identity.

Therefore, to evaluate the trust of service nodes scientifically, a new framework and evaluation method is needed to determine the weight of different indexes, and fully reflect the objectivity and accuracy of monitoring attributes. Instead, a whole evaluation framework of trust evaluation is required for CSCs' decision making, which can help them choose and monitor the operation state. In summary, current research of trust evaluation is still in its infancy, and there is yet a considerable problem space to explore and resolve. On the one hand, the influence factors are usually limited, which neglects the other factors which have an effect on trust. Novel trust establishment mechanisms that evaluate the trustworthiness of CIdPs have been advocated and provided (**Figure 2**). Likewise, to support the CIdUs in reliably identifying trustworthy CIdPs, a multi-faceted trust management system architecture for a CIdP is advocated. The concerns of evaluating cloud trust management systems, data gathering, and synthesis of theory and data, have been addressed so that the relationship between cloud identity providers and Cloud identity users can be improved.

Author details

Eghbal Ghazizadeh* and Brian Cusack

*Address all correspondence to: eghaziza@aut.ac.nz

Digital forensic Lab, Auckland University of Technology, New Zealand

References

[1] Blaze M, Feigenbaum J, Lacy J. Decentralized Trust Management. pp. 164-173

[2] Calheiros RN, Ranjan R, Beloglazov A, De Rose CA, Buyya R. CloudSim: A toolkit for modeling and simulation of cloud computing environments and evaluation of resource provisioning algorithms. Software: Practice and Experience. 2011;**41**(1):23-50

[3] Habib SM, Hauke S, Ries S, Mühlhäuser M. Trust as a facilitator in cloud computing: A survey. Journal of Cloud Computing. 2012;**1**(1):1-18

[4] Habiba U, Masood R, Shibli MA, Niazi MA. Cloud identity management security issues & solutions: A taxonomy. Complex Adaptive Systems Modeling. 2014;**2**(1):1-37

[5] Noor TH, Sheng QZ. Trust as a service: A framework for trust management in cloud environments. In: Web Information System Engineering–WISE 2011. Springer; 2011. pp. 314-321

[6] Al-Sharawneh J, Williams M. Credibility-Based Social Network Recommendation: Follow the Leader. pp. 1-11

[7] Alabool HM, Mahmood AKB. A novel evaluation framework for improving trust level of infrastructure as a service. Cluster Computing. 2015:1-22

[8] Lopez M. An Evaluation Theory Perspective of the Architecture Tradeoff Analysis Method (ATAM), DTIC Document. 2000

[9] Huang, Nicol DM. Trust mechanisms for cloud computing. Journal of Cloud Computing. 2013;**2**(1):1-14

[10] Samani R, Reavis J, Honan B. CSA Guide to Cloud Computing: Implementing Cloud Privacy and Security: Syngress. 2014

[11] Saleh ASA, Hamed EMR, Hashem M. Building Trust Management Model for Cloud Computing. pp. PDC-116-PDC-125

[12] Huang L, He X, Liao HD, Ji M. Developing a trustworthy computing framework for clouds. International Journal of Embedded Systems. 2016;**8**(1):59-68

[13] Wang L, Li X, Yan X, Qing S, Chen Y. Service dynamic trust evaluation model based on Bayesian network in distributed computing environment. Distributed Computing. 2015;**9**(5)

[14] Hallappanavar VL, Birje MN. Trust Management in Cloud Computing. Security Solutions for Hyperconnectivity and the Internet of Things. 2016:151

[15] Shaikh R, Sasikumar M. Trust model for measuring security strength of cloud computing service. Procedia Computer Science. 2015;**45**:380-389

[16] Chhabra S, Dixit VS. Cloud computing: State of the art and security issues. ACM SIGSOFT Software Engineering Notes. 2015;**40**(2):1-11

[17] NIST. NIST Cloud Computing Standards Roadmap. 2013

[18] Wu X, Zhang R, Zeng B, Zhou S. A trust evaluation model for cloud computing. Procedia Computer Science. 2013;**17**:1170-1177

[19] ABC4Trust, "Attribute-Based Credentials for Trust. European Union Funded Project of the 7th Framework Programme.," 2015

[20] Pecori R. S-Kademlia: A trust and reputation method to mitigate a Sybil attack in Kademlia. Computer Networks. 2016;**94**:205-218

[21] Alaqra A, Fischer-Hübner S, Groß T, Lorünser T, Slamanig D. Signatures for privacy, trust and accountability in the cloud: Applications and requirements. In: Privacy and Identity Management. Time for a Revolution? Springer; 2016. pp. 79-96

[22] Aguirre E, Mahr D, Grewal D, Ruyter de K, and Wetzels M, Unraveling the personalization paradox: The effect of information collection and trust-building strategies on online advertisement effectiveness. Journal of Retailing. 2015;**91**(1):34-49

[23] Zhang M, Huo B. The impact of dependence and trust on supply chain integration. International Journal of Physical Distribution & Logistics Management. 2013;**43**(7):544-563

[24] DiMaria J. CloudTrust Protocol Working Group; https://cloudsecurityalliance.org/group/cloudtrust-protocol/

[25] Alshehri MD, Hussain FK. A Comparative Analysis of Scalable and Context-Aware Trust Management Approaches for Internet of Things. pp. 596-605

[26] Noor TH, Sheng QZ, Zeadally S, Yu J. Trust management of services in cloud environments: Obstacles and solutions. ACM Computing Surveys (CSUR). 2013;**46**(1):12

[27] Noor TH, Sheng QZ, Maamar Z, Zeadally S. Managing Trust in the Cloud: State of the art and research challenges. Computer. 2016;**49**(2):34-45

[28] Luo, Liu J, Xiong J, Wang L. Defending against Whitewashing Attacks in Peer-To-Peer File-Sharing Networks. pp. 1087-1094

[29] Duncan A, Creese S, Goldsmith M. An overview of insider attacks in cloud computing. Concurrency and Computation: Practice and Experience. 2015;**27**(12):2964-2981

[30] Lehrig S, Eikerling H, Becker S. Scalability, Elasticity, and Efficiency in Cloud Computing: A Systematic Literature Review of Definitions and Metrics. pp. 83-92

[31] Pearson S. Privacy, security and trust in cloud computing. In: Privacy and Security for Cloud Computing. Springer; 2013. pp. 3-42

[32] Dane E, Rockmann KW, Pratt MG. When should I trust my gut? Linking domain expertise to intuitive decision-making effectiveness. Organizational Behavior and Human Decision Processes. 2012;**119**(2):187-194

[33] Messina F, Pappalardo G, Rosaci D, Sarné GM. A Trust-Based, Multi-Agent Architecture Supporting Inter-Cloud Vm Migration in Iaas Federations. pp. 74-83

[34] Jahani A, Khanli LM. Cloud service ranking as a multi objective optimization problem. The Journal of Supercomputing. 2016:1-30

[35] Sun D, Chang G, Sun L, Wang X. Surveying and analyzing security, privacy and trust issues in cloud computing environments. Procedia Engineering. 2011;**15**:2852-2856

[36] Corradini F, De Angelis F, Ippoliti F, Marcantoni F. A Survey of Trust Management Models for Cloud Computing. 2015

[37] Dondio P, Longo L. Trust-based techniques for collective intelligence in social search systems. In: Next Generation Data Technologies for Collective Computational Intelligence. Springer; 2011. pp. 113-135

[38] Hillary N, Madsen K. You cannot Control What you cannot Measure, OR why it's Close to Impossible to Guarantee Real-Time Software Performance on a CPU with on-Chip Cache

[39] Quinn SD, Souppaya M, Cook M, Scarfone K. National Checklist Program for IT products —Guidelines for checklist users and developers. NIST Special Publication. 2011;**800**:70

[40] Barreira I, Fiedler A, Miękina A, Wanko C, Górniak S. Auditing framework for TSPs, https://www.enisa.europa.eu/publications/tsp1-framework

[41] Hu VC, Kent KA. Guidelines for Access Control System Evaluation Metrics: Citeseer, 2012

[42] Dixon-Woods M, Cavers D, Agarwal S, Annandale E, Arthur A, Harvey J, Hsu R, Katbamna S, Olsen R, Smith L. Conducting a critical interpretive synthesis of the literature on access to healthcare by vulnerable groups. BMC Medical Research Methodology. 2006;**6**(1):1

[43] Dixon-Woods M. Using framework-based synthesis for conducting reviews of qualitative studies. BMC Medicine. 2011;**9**(1):1

[44] Gopinath PG, Vasudevan SK. An in-depth analysis and study of load balancing techniques in the cloud computing environment. Procedia Computer Science. 2015;**50**:427-432

[45] Moreno-Vozmediano R, Montero RS, Llorente IM. Key challenges in cloud computing: Enabling the future internet of services. Internet Computing, IEEE. 2013;**17**(4):18-25

[46] Iriberri A, Leroy G. A life-cycle perspective on online community success. ACM Computing Surveys (CSUR). 2009;**41**(2):11

[47] Khalid U, Ghafoor A, Irum M, Shibli MA. Cloud based secure and privacy enhanced authentication & authorization protocol. Procedia Computer Science. 2013;**22**:680-688

[48] Kshetri N. Privacy and security issues in cloud computing: The role of institutions and institutional evolution. Telecommunications Policy. 2013;**37**(4):372-386

[49] Arias-Cabarcos P, Almenárez-Mendoza F, Marín-López A, Díaz-Sánchez D, Sánchez-Guerrero R. A metric-based approach to assess risk for "on cloud" federated identity management. Journal of Network and Systems Management. 2012;**20**(4):513-533

[50] Djemame K, Armstrong D, Guitart J, Macias M. "A Risk Assessment Framework for Cloud Computing," 2014

[51] Theoharidou, Papanikolaou N, Gritzalis D. Privacy Risk, Security, Accountability in the Cloud. pp. 177-184

[52] Loutfi I, Jøsang A. Fido trust requirements. In: Secure IT Systems. Springer; 2015. pp. 139-155

[53] Zhu L, Tung B. "Public Key Cryptography for Initial Authentication in Kerberos (PKINIT). IETF," 2015

[54] Jyotiyana JP, Mishra A. Secure authentication: Eliminating possible backdoors in client-server endorsement. Procedia Computer Science. 2016;**85**:606-615

[55] Alsharnouby M, Alaca F, Chiasson S. Why phishing still works: User strategies for combating phishing attacks. International Journal of Human-Computer Studies. 2015;**82**:69-82

[56] OpenID. "RISC (risk and incident sharing and coordination) WG," http://openid.net/wg/risc/

[57] Leicher A, Schmidt AU, Shah Y. Smart OpenID: A Smart Card Based OpenID Protocol. pp. 75-86

[58] Li W, Mitchell CJ. Security Issues in OAuth 2.0 SSO Implementations. pp. 529-541

[59] Yan L, Rong C, Zhao G. Strengthen Cloud Computing Security with Federal Identity Management Using Hierarchical Identity-Based Cryptography. pp. 167-177

[60] Mahalle PN, Anggorojati B, Prasad NR, Prasad R. Identity authentication and capability based access control (iacac) for the internet of things. Journal of Cyber Security and Mobility. 2013;**1**(4):309-348

[61] Russell B. "Internet of things working group," https://cloudsecurityalliance.org/group/internet-of-things/

[62] Disterer G. "Iso/Iec 27000, 27001 and 27002 for Information Security Management," 2013

Chapter 4

Cloud Application Portability: Issues and Developments

Isaac Odun-Ayo, Chinonso Okereke and
Hope Orovwode

Additional information is available at the end of the chapter

http://dx.doi.org/10.5772/intechopen.75464

Abstract

Cloud computing is a standard that is fast gaining momentum in the IT world. The availability of storage capacity that can be accessed and increased as the need arises makes computing easier. Applications can also be deployed using services provided by a cloud service provider. Portability allows utilization of applications and services across various domains. Portability could be in the area of programming language, application programming interface, data storage or data migration. Clearly, the easier it is to move services across various providers, the more attractive cloud computing becomes. The study was executed by means of review of some literature available on cloud application portability. This chapter examines current trends in cloud application portability area and gives focus for future research. In the present work, the objective is to answer the following question: what is the current trend and development in cloud application portability? Papers published in journals, conferences, white papers, and reputable magazines were analyzed. Some core topic facets were used in this review for the identification of trends in cloud application portability. The finding is that discussions on virtualization and API-specific issues are not adequate. This will be of benefit to prospective cloud users and even cloud providers.

Keywords: cloud computing, Internet of Things, portability, data storage, APIs

1. Introduction

According to [1], cloud computing is a paradigm for enabling universal, easy-to-use, on-demand network access to a shared pool of configurable computing resources such as networks,

storage, servers, applications, and services, which can be quickly provided and released with very little management effort. Cloud service portability can be well-defined as the capacity to move cloud services from one provider to another in an easy manner. Cloud computing can also be described as "a large scale distributed computing model motivated by frugalities of scale in which a pool of abstracted, virtualized, dynamically scalable managed storage, computing power, services, and platforms are distributed on demand to external customers over the Internet" [2]. Important features of cloud computing are scalability, on-demand service, and virtualization. The virtualized resources are provided through an Application Programming Interface (API) [3]. Cloud computing offers three major services, namely, Software-as-a-Service (SaaS), Platform-as-a-Service (PaaS) and Infrastructure-as-a-Service (IaaS). Cloud deployment types are public, private, community, and hybrid clouds. Enterprises through cloud computing are able to focus on core activities and training instead of spending time and money on infrastructure.

Procurement of infrastructure is reduced or eliminated; it also implies little or no maintenance cost on infrastructure. On-demand benefit of the cloud ensures that enterprises utilize what they need per time, using state of the art technology. Importantly, only a resource utilized is paid for. In SaaS, a software that is owned, delivered, and managed remotely by one or more cloud service providers is offered on a pay-per-use manner [3]. SaaS usually is the most noticeable layer of cloud computing for cloud users. This is because it is majorly about actual software applications that are used and accessed on the cloud. IaaS refers to computing services like processing or storage that can be gotten as a service. The process of virtualization is the primary means of providing IaaS services. The PaaS referred to an abstraction layer between the IaaS and SaaS. PaaS is concerned with software development. Users develop their applications based on a platform and upload the code to the platform provided by the CSP. The user does not need to worry about infrastructure and the CSP manages the scaling of the applications. Applications deployed on the cloud including data are difficult to move between clouds, leading to portability issues. Vendor lock-in occurs when a cloud user cannot move data and application from a particular cloud service provider [4]. The lock-in could be termed vertical or horizontal heterogeneity [5]. Vertical heterogeneity occurs with IaaS that provides infrastructure to consumers. PaaS allows development and deployment of user's applications. Such a platform uses specialized libraries and routines and moving application to another platform will require extensive changes [5]. In view of this, cloud users are forced to remain with a particular CSP and porting becomes very expensive [5]. Portability will therefore mean that cloud users will write codes that work in different clouds irrespective of the nature of the clouds. However, this should not be strictly so. Consumers should be able to change CSPs and move to any CSP that offers a better service at possibly a lower cost. Unfortunately, different cloud application platform offerings are categorized by considerable heterogeneity [6]. In view of these irreconcilabilities, users who deploy an application to a specific platform may find it difficult moving such an application to another CSP.

The focus of this chapter is to scrutinize data and application portability in cloud computing. The issues involved in application portability are discussed. Current industry trends are also be examined. This chapter contributes to enhancing developments in the area of cloud application portability. The rest of the chapter is structured as follows: Section 2 examines related work. Section 3 discusses issues related to cloud portability. Section 4 highlights the current development in cloud portability with reference to developments in the industry. Section 5 concludes the chapter and suggests the future area of research.

2. Related work

In [5], cloud application portability: an initial view is presented. The focus is on examining the heterogeneous nature of cloud platforms. Approaches to tackling the identified challenges were proposed through a cross-platform application process. In [4], the need for portability and interoperability in cloud computing is proposed. The approach is an open source model for enhancing portability and interoperability in the various cloud platforms. This will eventually reduce the cost of cloud migration. In [7], semantics-centric solutions for application and data portability in cloud computing is presented. The focus is on the problem of data and application portability in the cloud. The semantic web community proposed some solutions to overcome some aspects of cloud portability. In [6], portable cloud services using Topology and Orchestration Specification for Cloud Applications (TOSCA) is proposed. The focus is on the possibility of moving services between cloud providers to avoid vendor lock-in. This was done at the managerial and operational level using TOSCA. In [8], a portable cloud application—from theory to practice—is presented. The approach was to design an open source application capable of handling multiple cloud usage. This helps to deal with the issues of application, data, and service portability on the cloud.

In [9], a comparative analysis of legislation on how to attribute the right to data portability in Europe is presented. It discussed how competition is prevented by cloud service providers through lock-in. Thereafter, it examines legislation that makes portability possible for cloud consumers. In [10], a new cloud services portability platform is proposed. The approach is to design a cloud portability framework using an adapter model. This approach leverages on TOSCA for application portability. In [11], application mobility in pervasive computing: a survey is presented. The focus is to examine different migration methods for application portability. A framework was proposed along four dimensions to allow easy mobility of applications. In [12], challenges emerging from future cloud application scenarios are presented. Various aspects of cloud computing were examined. The issues of integration and interoperability were also discussed and suggestions made on the way forward. In [13], enabling portability in advanced information-centric services over structured peer-to-peer systems is proposed. The approach is a three-layer architecture to enhance portability. The middleware in the framework is versatile over a wide variety of applications. In [14], streamlining DevOps automation for cloud application using TOSCA as standardized metamodel is presented. The chapter proposes a framework for integrating different applications on the cloud. The framework is also implemented and validated. In [15], toward application portability in platform as a service is presented. The approach was to discuss portability options in terms of PaaS provider and the ecosystem capabilities. The proposed model was implemented with a data set and different PaaS vendors.

3. Cloud portability issues

3.1. Layers of platform as a service

"Application portability is the capability of program to be implemented on numerous types of data processing systems without changing the program to a dissimilar language and with little or no modification" [4]. Portability is the capacity to use mechanisms or system lying on several software or hardware environments [8]. The primary focus of portability is in the PaaS. PaaS is divided into three layers namely, infrastructure, platform, and management. Since PaaS hides most of its physical properties, users are left with concepts like dynos, workers' units, gears, or app cells that can be used for specific instances in PaaS, while CPU and disk utilization are negligible [4]. The CPU usage is the main factor for billing in IaaS, but instances count and RAM size are used in PaaS. Geographical location of application deployment is another issue. Based on latency considerations, applications are also subject to regional regulations [4]. The platform constitutes the hosting environment with two stack components: the runtime stack and service stack [4].

The runtime stack in PaaS constitutes the programming language used for developing the application such as Ruby on Rails which is fairly popular [4]. Higher stack leads to the more specificity in the application dependency; hence increasing lock-in risk. The service stack is divided into add-one and native and add–on services. The latter services, which are native services, are hosted by PaaS vendors, and it includes latency and performance services like data store [4]. While Add-on service is provided by third parties: they include data store and services like analytics, search engines, and messaging services. Another aspect is extensibility involving build packs that enable developments add own packages of service. The management layers allow control of the deployed application which encompasses pushing, starting and stopping an application, including the provision of native and add-on services. Importantly, resource usage and monitoring necessary for billings and scaling decision is carried out at the management layer. Even though the mentioned functionalities are collectively used by all various PaaS to a large extent, commands and procedures are not standardized and vary broadly between providers [4].

3.2. Need, levels and advantages of application portability

Cloud portability guarantees that applications, data, or services work in the same way in different cloud services with a common programmable interaction [8]. A primary reason for portability is migrating all or part of existing services between clouds. This could be because of the need for optimal utilization, to reduce cost, technology, or SLA issues. Most challenging are situations in which a user's cloud application is distributed between two or more providers and administrative domain simultaneously [9]. Portability can be categorized into three ways: functional portability, data portability, and service enhancement. Functional portability is realized by describing the application's functionality details in a vendor–agnostic manner [8]. Device agnosticism allows hardware and software components to work with various systems without requiring any special adaptations. Hence, there is compatibility across most common systems. Data portability is reached when a customer is able to access and salvage application data from one provider and to input this into a corresponding application hosted by another provider. Service enhancements metadata is added through annotation [8]. The metadata provides information about other data. Also, control APIs permit infrastructure to be added and reconfigured instantaneously, based on traffic and other factors [9]. The requirement for portability at PaaS focuses on lessening the amount of rewriting when application is ported. Data portability permits users to transfer their personal information from one service to another, choosing a service suitable to their needs [10]. Another advantage of porting is that it allows a user to be released from lock-in to a provider. Ironically, data portability is also in the interest of the CSP. This is because when users are allowed to freely move data, trust will be enhanced between CSPs and users. In addition, more information can be used by CSPs in the area of advertising.

3.3. Areas of challenge in application portability

There are four areas of concern in application portability, namely programming language and framework, platform-specific services, data store, and platform-specific configuration files [11]. The specific programming language that is used to build an application is a major determining factor in cross-platform deployment. All cloud platforms have certain languages and framework which they support. For instance, Google AppEngine makes available support to Java, but does not extend such support to Java class libraries which are supported by OpenShift [11]. Cloud platform provides services through specific APIs. A service is a high–level functionality that the provider can use with no need for from-scratch implementation [6]. Analytical tools that are used in data sets and APIs for image manipulation are examples in this area. Reduction of application development time can be achieved when developers use such platform services. Developers can join in functionalities from platform services by binding it to the respective platform APIs instead of programming those functionalities from scratch [8].

Two types of data storage exist on the cloud platform. These are: data base store and file store. Data base store is for strong structured data, while file store is like a hard disk on the cloud. There are two kinds of data base store: SQL and NoSQL. The SQL database is the traditional relational database available on all major cloud providers. The NoSQL is a new system that groups all database systems that do not adhere to the SQL relational structure. NoSQL has simple operations, faster access, and the ability to distribute data over many services among other characteristics [6].

Configuration files are used by traditional software applications to instruct the environment on how to execute on the application. Platform-specific configuration files also exist on the cloud. Google AppEngine, for instance, uses the "app engine – web xml" file. Adapting the configuration file to each target cloud platform affects application portability [8]. Solution to cloud portability issues are through standardization and intermediation. Standardization indicates the definition of common set of standards for PaaS offerings. The adaption of such standards by all CSPs will enable developers design, deploy, and manage their applications independent of a cloud platform.

The Distributed Management Task Force (DMTF) evolved the open virtualization format (OVF) that enables standardization of virtual machines' formats and portability. The Storage Network Industry Associations (SNIA) evolved the Cloud Data Management Interface (CDMI) to standardize the issue of cloud storage services [5]. The Topology and Orchestration Specification for Cloud Applications (TOSCA) is supported by Organization for the Advancement of Structured Information Standards (OASIS) for standardizing applications to enable portability across platforms [5]. Intermediation frees application development from platform-specific APIs and supported formats. jCloud and mOSAIC are open source platforms meant to resolve portability issues based on platform-specific APIs [5]. The issue of data storage is also being addressed by the Bridge Query Language (BQL).

4. Industry perspective in cloud portability

As already discussed, several organizations have emerged to deal with the issue of portability. To move workloads between clouds, there is a need for standardized programming interfaces, layers of abstraction, and management capabilities [4]. Making programming interfaces standard allows movement of programs between interfaces. These standards allow companies to leverage on toolsets when preparing IT tasks for deployment on a cloud service [4]. Portability between cloud resources is also made more feasible by insulation of cloud services from underlying infrastructure through layer of abstraction. Layer of abstraction also increases speed of switching cloud services as well as decreases the cost and stress of such activity because of a reduction in the dependency on underlying infrastructure like processors, operating system and virtualization software [4]. Management capability is necessary to enable IT personnel handle the cloud services to which they subscribe without the introduction of new layers of capability. For success, these management capabilities must work well with already existing management products, both for managing virtual and physical services.

4.1. Support for multiple hypervisor technology

Multiple hypervisor technology such as VMware, Hyper-V, KVM Ven should be supported appropriately [4]. The virtual machine has become an essential unit of work and encapsulation especially for IaaS and some PaaS clouds [4]. Support for multiple hypervisor technology should enable customers choose their preferred VM and quickly transfer to it irrespective of the underlying platform. This is because there is likely to be mixed virtualization environment in the enterprise of a customer.

4.2. Choice of operating system

The coming of application virtualization continues to break the ties between the operating system and the application but a large number of applications are still dependent on specific versions of an operating system [4]. Enterprises have built several types of operating systems in their data centers overtime; which implies that it is impossible to limit users of the cloud to only a particular type of OS (Operating System) and enterprises would not be able to attend to large number of workloads.

4.3. Programming models

Data centers were chosen by most enterprises a long time ago and some of these programming models may not be right for the cloud. IT staff could also show reluctance to change these programming models because of their familiarity with them [4]. Cloud providers must utilize current programming models such as. Net and Java, and web models like PHP and Ruby. When clouds do not support these languages, more importance is placed on hybrid cloud management.

4.4. Application programming interface

PaaS cloud is simply programming to a given cloud platform. PaaS has a lot of functionalities such as massive scalability. On the other hand, APIs are useful only to new applications. There is a need for the modification of existing applications to benefit from these APIs. This modification is usually difficult and expensive procedure [4]. In effect, customers must examine the complete API set in such a way as to be able to migrate and also move out later if the need arises. Although cloud service providers are excited about migrating customers to their platform and usually provide tools for this purpose, it is sometimes difficult for customers to move their applications from cloud to cloud [4].

4.5. Unified management

Dedicated management console is a vital part of every cloud technology including public clouds. This management must aim for more unification. This is especially because of the need for tighter coordination between on-premises and off-premises resources in a hybrid cloud [4]. API and management data accessibility would allow unified cloud console to support access control, scheduling, resource management, and billing.

4.6. Data portability

The data on application must also be portable, not just in terms of copying files from one location to another. Data can exist in the form of database or file with varying access methods. Data portability means application would be able to access and move production data which they need to operate upon [4]. Enterprise data requires appropriate standards for the support of data export and conversion from one format to another.

4.7. License flexibility

Software licensing has always been bound to location and hardware, and this has not changed with cloud computing. Customers must know of the restriction that software license has on cloud portability [4].

4.8. Topology and orchestration specification for cloud applications

TOSCA defines composite applications and how they are managed using modules and for portability [6]. It characterizes the service template that contains a cloud service topology and its operations. For example, it defines an application hosted on an server which is hosted on an operating system, and method of deployment, method of termination, and management of the services provided [6]. Typically, managing services requires a lot of manual effort by the customer. Each enterprise learns how to operate an application, acquires management knowledge, and automates certain aspects in the scripts. TOSCA solves this challenge by enabling application development and operators to model management best practice and reoccurring tasks into clear plans [6]. With these plans being por between different environments and providers, reusability and automation of service management is achieved and this reduces the total ownership cost by a significant percentage. Automated service management will also enhance rapid elasticity and self-service. TOSCA plan is portable specifically because of its workflow language and engines it uses [6]. Example of workflow languages portable between dissimilar engines are Business Process Model and Notation (BPMN) and Business Process Expression Language (BPEL).

5. Analysis and discussion

Cloud portability is a topic with huge importance to cloud computing. This section analyses some of the most recent research papers based on some core areas namely virtualization

References	Virtualization issue	Data issues	Applications issues	API issues	Identity management and access control	Security concerns	Interoperability
[17]			x	x			
[18]	x	x	x			x	
[21]	x	x	x	x		x	x
[26]	x		x				x
[27]			x				x
[28]							
[22]	x		x			x	x
[23]	x		x			x	x
[19]	x	x		x		x	x
[24]	x	x	x			x	x
[29]	x		x	x			x
[30]			x	x			x
[16]			x				
[31]			x	x			x
[20]		x		x	x		

Table 1. Comparative analysis of cloud portability issues.

issues, data portability, application/application portability issues, API issues, security concerns, identity management/access control, and interoperability issues. **Table 1** shows the comparative analysis of the core areas in cloud portability. From the analysis of the reviewed papers, application portability issues is seen to be the most discussed as it is mentioned in all reviewed papers except [16]. In contrast to application portability, only 33% of the reviewed papers specifically dealt with data portability issues. This is because application portability is more significant that data portability. Next highly mentioned with 87% among the reviewed papers are interoperability issues. These are because cloud portability and interoperability issues usually go hand in hand. Only [17–20] did not discuss interoperability issues. Virtualization and API-specific issues were averagely discussed with 53% each. However only [16, 18, 21–25], that is, 40% of the reviewed papers, addressed security concerns. The lowest researched area from recently reviewed papers is identity management/access control issues which was only mentioned in [22]. It shows its minimal significance in cloud portability.

Based on the analysis, most of the mentioned core areas were researched based on their perceived significance. However, the suggestion is for more focused research on security concerns in cloud portability-related researches. It is also noted that more research can be carried out to address virtualization and API issues. Identity management/access control issues in cloud portability can be of importance going forward and needs to be focused on a little more.

6. Conclusion

Cloud computing and application portability are vital issues in the cloud. Users are exposed to lock-in because of the inherent challenges of data and application portability. This is usually more pronounced in PaaS cloud, especially in terms of infrastructure and platform. Portability issues in term of APIs, storage, programming languages, and configuration files were discussed. There are organizations creating solutions to allow for standardization and intermediation in cloud portability. Suggestion from the industry was also examined and TOSCA (meant for application portability) was briefly discussed. In view of its relevance to cloud portability, discussions on virtualization and API-specific issues must continue to evolve.

Acknowledgements

We acknowledge the support and sponsorship provided by Covenant University through the Centre for Research, Innovation, and Discovery (CUCRID).

Author details

Isaac Odun-Ayo*, Chinonso Okereke and Hope Orovwode

*Address all correspondence to: isaac.odun-ayo@covenantuniversity.edu.ng

Covenant University, Ota, Nigeria

References

[1] Mell P, Grance T. The NIST Definition of Cloud Computing Recommendations of the National Institute of Standards and Technology. National Institute of Standards and Technology, Information Technology Laboratory. 2011;**145**:7. https://doi.org/10.1136/emj.2010.096966

[2] Foster I, Zhao Y, Raicu I, Lu S. Cloud computing and grid computing 360-degree compared. In: Grid Computing Environments Workshop (GCE'08); 2008. DOI: 10.1109/GCE.2008.4738445

[3] Stanoevska-Slabeva K, Wozniak T. Grid and Cloud Computing: A Business Perspective on Technology and Applications. Heidelberg/Dordrecht/London/New York: Springer; 2010. ISBN: 978-3-642-0 e-ISBN 978-3-642-05193-7. DOI: 10.1007/978-3-642-05193-7

[4] Bozman J. Cloud Computing: The Need for Portability and Interoperability. IDC Executive Insights. www.idc.com/gms; 2010

[5] Gonidis F, Paraskakis I, Simons AJH, Kourtesis D. Cloud application portability: An initial view. BCI'13; September 19-21, 2013. ACM. 978-1-4503-1851-8/13/09

[6] Binz T, Breiter G, Leyman F, Spatzier T. Portable Cloud Services Using TOSCA. IEEE Internet Computing. Vol. 16. no. 3. pp. 80-85. May-June 2012. DOI: 10.1109/MIC.2012.43 http://doi.ieeecomputersociety.org/10.1109/MIC.2012.43

[7] Ranabahu AH, Sheth AP. Semantics centric solutions for application and data portability in cloud computing. In: Proceedings of the IEEE Second International Conference on Cloud Computing Technology and Science; 2010. pp. 234-241. http://corescholar.libraries.wright.edu/knoesis/766

[8] Petcu D, Macariu G, Panica S, Cráciun C. Portable cloud application-from theory to practice. Future Generation Computer Systems. 2012;**29**(2013):1417-1430

[9] Van der Auwermeulen B. How to attribute the right to data portability in Europe: A comparative analysis of legislations. Computer Law & Security Review. 2017;**33**(2017):57-72

[10] Kostoska M, Gusev M, Ristov S. A new cloud services portability platform. In: 24th DAAAM International Symposium on Intelligent Manufacturing and Automation 2013; 2014

[11] Yu P, Ma X, Cao J, Lu J. Application mobility in pervasive computing: A survey. Pervasive and Mobile Computing. 2012, 2013;**9**:2-17

[12] Jeferry K, Kousiouris G, Kyriazis D, Altmann J, Ciuffoletti A, Maglogiannis I, Nes P, Suzic B, Zhao Z. Challenges emerging from future cloud application scenarios. Procedia Computer Science. 2015;**68**(2015):227-237

[13] Pujo-Ahulló J, López PG. Enabling portability in advanced information centric services over structured peer-to-peer systems. Journal of Network and Computer Applications. 2010;**33**(2010):556-568

[14] Wettinger J, Bietentúcher U, Kopp O, Leymann F. Streamlining DevOps automation for cloud application using Tosca as standardized metamodel. Future Generation Computer Systems. 2016;**56**(2016):317-332

[15] Kolb S, Wirtz G. Towards Application Portability in Platform as a Service. In: Proceedings of the 2014 IEEE 8th International Symposium on Service Oriented System Engineering (SOSE '14). Washington, DC, USA: IEEE Computer Society; 2014. pp. 218-229. DOI=http://dx.doi.org/10.1109/SOSE.2014.26

[16] Martino BD, Cretella G, Esposito A. Classification and Positioning of Cloud Definitions and Use Case Scenarios for Portability and Interoperability. Rome: 3rd International Conference on Future Internet of Things and Cloud; 2015. pp. 538-544. DOI: 10.1109/FiCloud.2015.119

[17] Munisso R, Chis AE. CloudMapper: A Model-Based Framework for Portability of Cloud Applications Consuming PaaS Services. 25th Euromicro International Conference on Parallel. St. Petersburg: Distributed and Network-based Processing (PDP); 2017. pp. 132-139. DOI: 10.1109/PDP.2017.94

[18] Pozdniakova O, MaZeika D. A Cloud Software Isolation and Cross-Platform Portability Methods. Open Conference of Electrical, Electronic and Information Sciences (eStream). Vilnius; 2017. pp. 1-6. DOI: 10.1109/eStream.2017.7950315

[19] Martino BD, Cretella G, Esposito A. Advances in Applications Portability and Services Interoperability among Multiple Clouds. In: IEEE Cloud Computing; Vol. 2. no. 2. pp. 22-28. Mar.-Apr. 2015. DOI: 10.1109/MCC.2015.38

[20] Brinkley J, Hoffman D, Tabrizi N. A Social Networking Site Portable Profile System for Blind and Visually Impaired Users Based on Cloud and Semantic Web Technologies. Honolulu, HI: IEEE International Conference on Cognitive Computing (ICCC); 2017. pp. 104-111. DOI: 10.1109/IEEE.ICCC.2017.21

[21] Parameswaran AV, Asheesh C. Cloud Interoperability and Standardization. In: SETLabs Briefings. 2009;**7**(7):19-27

[22] Moravčík M, Segeč P, Papán J, Hrabovský J. Overview of Cloud Computing and Portability Problems. 15th International Conference on Emerging eLearning Technologies and Applications (ICETA). Stary Smokovec; 2017. pp. 1-6. DOI: 10.1109/ICETA.2017.8102511

[23] Antoniades D et al. Enabling Cloud Application Portability. IEEE/ACM 8th International Conference on Utility and Cloud Computing (UCC). Limassol; 2015. pp. 354-360. DOI: 10.1109/UCC.2015.56

[24] Scandurra P, Psaila G, Capilla R, Mirandola R. Challenges and Assessment in Migrating IT Legacy Applications to the Cloud. IEEE 9th International Symposium on the Maintenance and Evolution of Service-Oriented and Cloud-Based Environments (MESOCA). Bremen, Germany: 2015. pp. 7-14. DOI: 10.1109/MESOCA.2015.7328120

[25] Atayero AA, Ilori OA, Adedokun MO. Cloud security and the Internet of Things: Impact on the virtual learning environment. In: Edulearn15 7th International Conference on Education and New Learning Technologies; 2015. pp. 3857-3863

[26] Martino BD, Esposito A, Cretella G. Semantic representation of cloud patterns and services with automated reasoning to support cloud application portability. IEEE Transactions on Cloud Computing. 2017;**5**(4):765-779

[27] Martino BD, Cretella G, Esposito A. Semantic and Agnostic Representation of Cloud Patterns for Cloud Interoperability and Portability. IEEE 5th International Conference on Cloud Computing Technology and Science. Bristol; 2013. pp. 182-187. DOI: 10.1109/CloudCom.2013.123

[28] Yangui S, Glitho RH, Wette C. Approaches to end-user applications portability in the cloud: A survey. IEEE Communications Magazine. 2016;**54**:138-145

[29] Markoska E, Kostoska M, Ristov S, Gusev M. Using P-TOSCA to prevent vendor lock-in for cloud-based laboratories. 23rd Telecommunications Forum Telfor (TELFOR). Belgrade; 2015. pp. 982-985. DOI: 10.1109/TELFOR.2015.7377629

[30] Kolb S, Röck C. Unified Cloud Application Management. IEEE World Congress on Services (SERVICES). San Francisco, CA; 2016. pp. 1-8. DOI: 10.1109/SERVICES.2016.7

[31] Markoska E, Chorbev I, Ristov S, Gusev M. Cloud Portability Standardization Overview. 38th International Convention on Information and Communication Technology, Electronics and Microelectronics (MIPRO). Opatija; 2015. pp. 286-291. DOI: 10.1109/MIPRO.2015.7160281

Chapter 5

Using Cloud Computing in Financial Institutions in Russia

Alexey V. Bataev

Additional information is available at the end of the chapter

http://dx.doi.org/10.5772/intechopen.75389

Abstract

The modern economy is developing under the influence of information and communication technologies. Cloud computing, Big Data, cyberphysical systems, here is an incomplete list of new directions, which with huge success is seen in every sphere of management and economy. This chapter deals with innovative ways of development connected with the use of cloud computing in the financial sphere. The history of occurrence and the basic preconditions in the development of cloud technology are analyzed. The major stages of the adoption of cloud computing in world development are considered. The main characteristics of cloud computing are explored: the types of clouds and methods of their provision are presented. The analysis of the Russian cloud technology market is carried out, the basic features and tendencies are revealed, and the further ways of development are defined. The evaluation of the possibility of using cloud computing in the financial institutions of the Russian Federation is given.

Keywords: IT technologies, cloud computing, types of clouds, kinds of cloud services, income of the Russian cloud computing market, cloud services in financial institutions, growth rate of cloud computing, cloud automated banking systems, advantages of cloud computing implementation

1. Introduction

In 2008, the financial and economic crisis began in the form of a strong reduction of the main economic indicators in most advanced economies, which later grew into a global recession (slowing) economy in the world.

The appearance of the crisis was associated with a number of factors: the general cyclical economic development; overheating of the credit market and the mortgage crisis, which was its consequence; high commodity prices (including oil); and overheating of the stock market.

The mortgage crisis in the USA, which in early 2007 affected the high-risk mortgages, was the predecessor of the 2008 financial crisis. The second wave of the mortgage crisis occurred in 2008, spreading to the standard segment, where banks issued loans refinanced by the state mortgage corporations. Owing to 20% fall in real estate prices, the American owners of housing lost nearly 5 trillion dollars.

In September 2008, the US mortgage crisis provoked the crisis of liquidity banks in the world: banks stopped lending. The crisis threw from banking sphere on real economy, began a recession, and a decline in production.

The global economic recession has resulted in the most developed world economies: the USA, China, and European Union experienced a complicated economic environment. The downturn in industrial production and a full-scale crisis in the financial sector are forced to look for new economic solutions in difficult conditions.

The crisis particularly showed up in the banking sector; financial institutions faced the problem of lowering the cost of doing business. Banks should search for a new innovative model of development; one of these areas could be one of the achievements of the information economy—cloud computing.

For the past 10 years, the topic of cloud computing has gained widespread interest not only among IT professionals but also in business. Cloud services began to take a leading role in the Russian market; they are looking narrowly not only at the big players but also at small and medium-sized businesses. Nowadays, the Russian market of cloud technologies constitutes billions of rubles. More Russian banks do not only discuss the prospects of these technologies but also actively introduce them into their business processes. Such major players in the banking business such as PJSC "Sberbank of Russia," JSC "VTB Bank," and JSC "Alfa-Bank" are actively investing in the cloud.

The implementation of cloud technology to the Russian market has their own specifics, connected both with problems in the law and with imperfect Internet access technologies, hardware and software, and limitations in financial opportunities.

2. Key research findings

2.1. The concept of cloud computing and the stages of development

Cloud computing is a technology of the distributed data processing in which computer resources and power are provided to the user as Internet service. The cloud service represents special client–server technology; a client uses resources (processor time, random access memory, disk space, network channels, specialized controllers, the software, etc.), a group of servers in network interacting in such a way that

- all groups look at the single virtual server for the client;
- the client can transparently and with high flexibility modify the volume of consumed resources in case of changes in their needs (increase/decrease server power with corresponding change of payment for it) [1–12].

The way of cloud computing development was difficult and long. For the first time, the idea of computing virtualization emerged under the optimization of large computers (mainframe) in the 1950s of the last century. At that time, the main problem was to provide maximum load of computers to cut downtime of computing power. The idea of providing temporary remote user access to the mainframe for a possibility of fully loaded computers arose just then.

The progress of personal computers led to a move away from expensive mainframe toward low-cost servers, so the subsequent development of cloud computing technology is not received.

An announcement from John McCarthy, that "the computing power could ever be publicly available resources" and the release of the book "The Challenge of the Computer Utility" by Douglas Parhilla in 1966, in which he described almost all the main characteristics of the existing clouds today, became the following important stage in the history of the concept of cloud computing (Microsoft Windows Azure: Information).

For the first time, the idea of what we now call cloud computing was announced by J.C.R. Licklider in 1970. During these years, he was responsible for the creation of Advanced Research Projects Agency Network (ARPAnet). His idea was that every person on Earth would be connected to the network, from which people receive not only data but also the program. Another scientist, John McCarthy, expressed the idea that computing power would be provided to users as a service [13, 14].

In 90 years, there was rapid development of the global Internet, which had an indirect impact on the development of cloud computing. Network capacity significantly increased and the coverage of geography expanded. Along with computer networks development, the hardware technologies were improved, multi-core processors appeared, and the volume of information warehouses considerably increased. All this has resulted in the development of computer technology, which provides the possibility of cloud services as follows:

- virtualization—process of remote access to computational capabilities;
- ASP—technology for creating web applications and web services;
- SOA—service-oriented architecture for the use of independent services with well-defined interfaces which can be called by some standard way for execution of the tasks;
- Web 2.0—the technique of designing systems that through taking the network interactions into consideration becomes better the more people use them;
- development framework—software development environment multiagent systems and applications;

- the distributed scalable computation—a way to solve time-consuming computational problems by using several computers, often combined in a parallel computing system;
- grid computing is a form of distributed computing whereby a "virtual supercomputer" is presented in the form of clusters connected by a network of loosely coupled, heterogeneous computers working together to perform a huge number of tasks (operations, works);
- utility computing is a service when the service of execution of particularly complex calculations or data storage arrays is ordered;
- open-source software—the source code of the programs available for viewing, study, and change that allows the user to take part in the finalization of the open program, use the code to create new programs, and fix errors in them [15, 16].

The further development of cloud computing technology continued in the middle of the 2000s. Amazon launched a service called Elastic Compute cloud (EC2) in 2006. This web service allowed the users to start up their own applications. Such giants of IT industry as Google, Sun, and IBM offered their cloud services a year later.

In 2008, Microsoft proposed not just a service but also a complete Windows Azure cloud operating system, which currently is one of the largest and most all-embracing projects in the field of cloud services.

In 2010, there were cloud services that were oriented not just to software developers but to simple users.

At the present time, there are three stages of cloud technologies development, suggested by the company "Gartner" (**Table 1**) [15].

The first stage is cloud computing developed by companies in which cloud technology attracted the ability to quickly enter the market and radically improve development efficiency. At this point, cloud computing was the most effective within IT projects, providing a return of investment for 18–24 months.

The main feature of the second phase is market consolidation. The number of cloud proposals exceeded the market needs. The struggle for users among different cloud vendors reached a peak, which led to a series of mergers and acquisitions. At the same time, the cloud offers

Stage	Duration, years	Comments
First projects	2007–2011	Cloud computing is implemented by companies that are willing to take risks.
Market consolidation	2010–2013	People are beginning to pay attention to cloud computing; growing competition and declines the total number of suppliers.
Mass distribution	2012–2015	Cloud computing is becoming the dominant trend; a limited number of suppliers dominate the market.

Table 1. Development stages of cloud computing.

increased and conservative users began to consider the possibility of using cloud computing seriously. The duration of cloud projects rose, and companies launched projects providing a return of investments for the period from 3 to 5 years.

According to prognosis, the accumulation of a critical mass and the mass distribution of cloud computing would come in the third stage. A small number of key suppliers who get an opportunity to offer the market its technology as de facto standards would dominate the market. The understanding of the risks associated with a dependence on specific cloud technology vendors would also grow. It would lead to a rise in popularity of a cloud-based platform with open source [15].

2.2. The main categories of cloud computing

It is possible to carry the following characteristics to the key parameters describing cloud computing:

- pooled resources: clouds very often represent big virtualized infrastructure, but it uses virtualization with functionality addition. Cloud technologies pool resources together and permit the automatic services working in the real mode to dynamically expand and scale user and service resources;
- self service: after the user uses the allocated resources, it should be given the opportunity to manage with the help of self-service mechanisms, for example, in order to transform them to configurations that are more profitable. The cloud-based resources are actually controlled by the user, who has all the possibilities to build them under the requirements;
- elastic—the elasticity of cloud technology is the ability to dynamically scale which is requested in a very short period of time by the user;
- usage-based—model postpaid use is a set of regulations that determine cloud services that the user pays only when using the power provided. It allows reconfiguring the resources, which are used, for example, to pay for the support and maintenance of idle equipment, to solve problems faced by corporation, thereby ensuring the effective use of resources.

The economic benefit is obvious: combining resources into a single unit; allowing to provide the necessary configuration with the possibility of optimal payment and allowing to build the infrastructure, through which the organization can solve economic problems facing it.

At present, there are three main methods of cloud services:

- Infrastructure as a service (Iaas)—the user is given an "empty" virtual server with a unique IP address or a set of Internet addresses and the information storage system. For the management of characteristics, start, and a server stop the provider accommodates the user with the program interface (API).
- Software as a service (Saas)—The SaaS concept enables the user to apply the software application as a service remotely through the Internet. This service does not buy expensive software but is just temporarily used to solve problems.

- Platform as a service (PaaS)—the users are made available to the virtual platform, consisting of one or more virtual servers with pre-installed operating systems and specialized applications. As a result, the user can choose from cloud services, one that is necessary for the decision of business problem.

The following cloud services differ within the focus areas:

- Hardware as a service (HaaS)—the user is provided with the equipment that he/she can use for his/her own purposes. An advantage is cost savings on the maintenance of the equipment and the need of its purchase is excluded. This variant is essentially a kind of IaaS service, characterized in that a user on the basis of the provided equipment may expand his/her own infrastructure with the necessary software.
- Workplace as a service (WaaS)—the customer uses the cloud for the creation of workplaces of employees, configures and installs all the necessary software for personnel work.
- Data as a service (DaaS)—the user is made available to disk space, on which he/she can store large amounts of information.
- Security as a service—the customer quickly installs security systems, ensuring the safe use of web technologies and reliable protection of the local network. This service saves on the expansion of own security.

The line between the methods of cloud services is quite thin, and very often the service is the synthesis of several services at the same time. Therefore, combining all services into one which received the name Everything as a Service (EaaS) has a tendency for the last time. In this case, the user is provided with all the software, hardware, and business process management, including interaction between users; the user needs only Internet access.

There are three types of clouds:

- private cloud—a secure IT infrastructure, controlled and exploited by one organization. The company can independently manage cloud or entrust it to an external organization, and the infrastructure can be located on the territory of the company, the vendor, or mixed. The private cloud deployed on the territory of the organization and fully managed by its employees is best variant;
- public cloud—an information infrastructure, which is also used by many companies. Users of public cloud only receive access to needed services, but are not able to manage, while they have no requirement to maintain infrastructure. Any company or an individual can become the user of this cloud. Owners of public clouds propose an easy and affordable way to deploy the required business systems and large possibilities of expansion;
- hybrid cloud—an infrastructure using the best quality of public and private clouds, in dealing with the task. Most often, this approach is used in companies having their own private cloud infrastructure, but in the case of a growth in their workload, a part of problems spreads to the public cloud, for example, large amounts of information [13, 17, 18].

2.3. Advantages of cloud computing

The use of cloud services has a number of advantages over using a conventional infrastructure:

- the user pays only for the amount of services that it needs and at the same time when there is such a requirement;
- cloud technologies allow for savings in the acquisition, maintenance, and upgrading of software and hardware;
- scalability—the ability to expand the number of servers, applications, and workplaces;
- fault tolerance—ensuring reliable operation of the system that can be duplicated when using cloud services;
- remote access—provides a possibility of access actually anywhere in the world where the Internet is available.

Along with the advantages, cloud services have several disadvantages:

- the user is not the owner (if the cloud is not completely private) and does not have access to cloud infrastructure; accordingly, the safety of the used data is completely dependent on the company, providing data services;
- to provide high-quality services required for high-speed Internet;
- absence of common standards in the field of cloud services security [12].

2.4. The global cloud computing market

Nowadays, the development of cloud computing occupies a large niche in the field of information technology. According to the prognosis of analytical company Forrester Research, the global cloud computing market would reach 241 billion dollars by 2020 (**Figure 1**), and the market of cloud applications and services available through the Internet would grow to 159.3 billion dollars by that time (**Figure 2**) [19–21]. At the same time, the average annual growth in the cloud computing and services market would exceed 20%.

2.5. Analysis of the Russian cloud computing market

Cloud technologies are developing very rapidly in Russia. According to the research by Orange Business Services analysts, the income of the Russian cloud services market amounted to 19 billion rubles for business in 2016. In parallel with this, the services market on the creation of cloud infrastructure brought more than 20 billion rubles of income. At the same time, the average annual growth was over 50% [22–25].

The market of services based on building cloud infrastructure exceeds the volume of the cloud services market in 2016. It became possible, thanks to the rapid growth of the amount of services in a construction of "clouds," their merge and customization, and movement from conventional infrastructure to cloud one. In total, the share of cloud services is expected to reach 13% of the Russian market of IT services by 2017 [26–31].

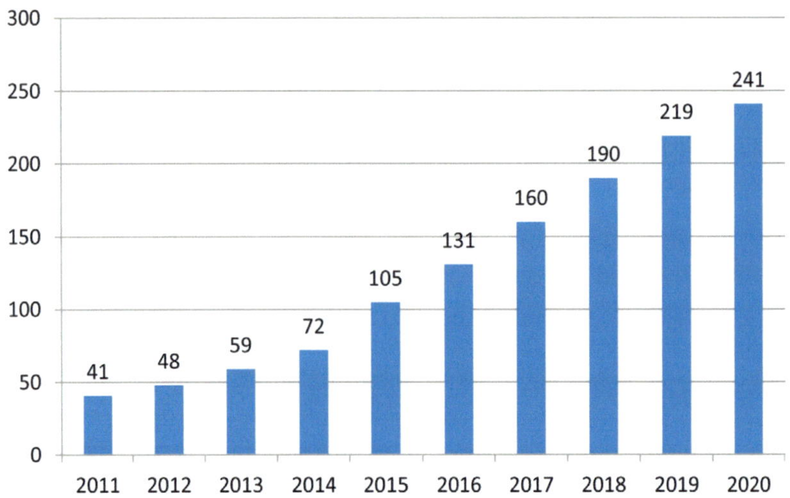

Figure 1. Volume of the world market of cloud computing, billion dollars.

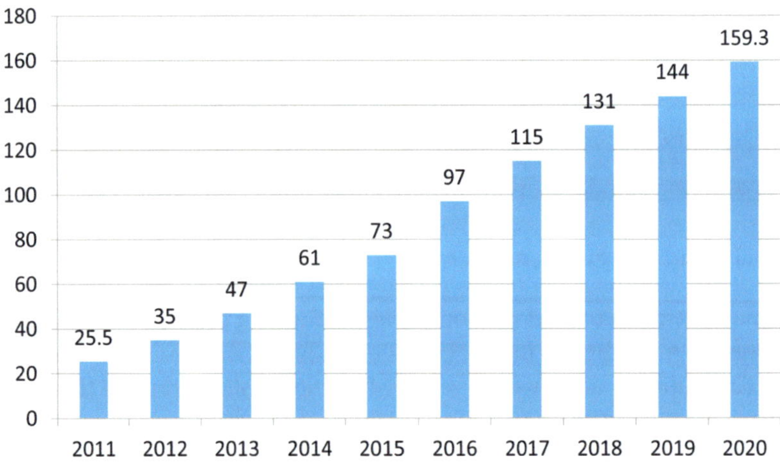

Figure 2. The global market of cloud-based applications and services, billion dollars.

If we consider the dynamics of the Russian market of cloud computing, it is much higher than the global growth rate (**Table 2**). This is explained by the fact that the Russian market lags behind the global cloud computing market and has to be hastened to catch up.

Despite the shortcomings of cloud, perspectives of their introduction are huge in Russia. According to Orange Business Services research, the income of the Russian market of cloud services for business has increased from 4.5 billion rubles in 2012 to 19 billion rubles in 2016 (**Figure 3**). At the same time with this, the service market to build cloud infrastructure brought more than 20 billion rubles of profit. Moreover, the service market based on the creation of cloud infrastructure exceeded the size of the market of cloud services in 2016. It became possible, thanks to the rapid growth in the volume of services for the construction of clouds, their

	2013 (%)	2014 (%)	2015 (%)	2016 (%)
The dynamics of the world cloud infrastructure market	23	25	45	25
The dynamics of the world cloud services market	34	22	13	32
The dynamics of the Russian cloud infrastructure market	75	43	41	32
The dynamics of the Russian cloud services market	81	59	48	37

Table 2. Comparative indicators of cloud services for the Russian market with the world, author development.

merge and customization, and movement from conventional infrastructure to cloud one. In total, the share of cloud services is expected to reach 13% of all Russian markets of IT services by 2017 [26, 30, 31].

The decisions in the IaaS infrastructure are most preferred for Russian customers. This kind of service is the most demanded, and the annual growth of these services is about 40% (**Figure 4**). It is explained by the desire of clients to administer the systems independently that is caused by feature of the Russian market, a large number of programs of own development, and also the general mistrust of customers to the cloud computing market. At the present time, 11 major players represent IaaS market: ActiveCloud, Clodo, Cloud One, Croc, Parking.ru (Group Inoventica), Selectel, "I-Teco," "Oversun," "Scalaxi," Cloud4Y, and Dataline (**Figure 5**). The penetration of IaaS was about 4% in Moscow and St. Petersburg, in other regions, less than 1% at the beginning of 2013 [27, 28].

Software SaaS is the second most important service in the field of cloud computing. It shows an annual growth of 50% and in the future will only increase the volume according to analysts' prognosis (**Figure 4**). There are five main players on the Russian SaaS service market, who occupy more than 90% of all markets (**Figure 6**).

The use of PaaS services, which is not very popular in Russia, is the next step in the development of the cloud market; however, the first proposals from the foreign supplier began to appear. According to different estimates, the market size of PaaS and BPaaS (business

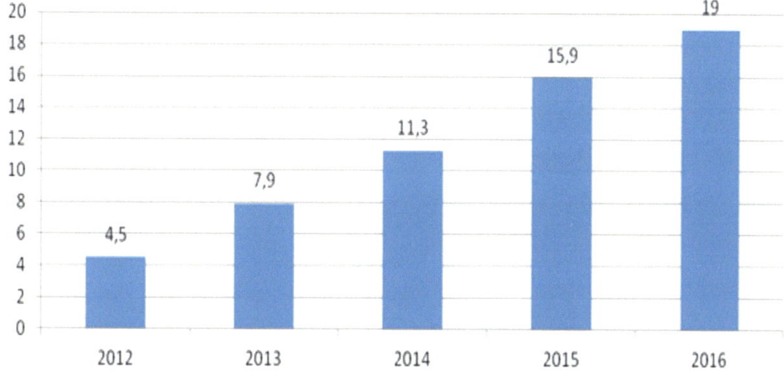

Figure 3. The volume of the Russian market of cloud services, billion rubles.

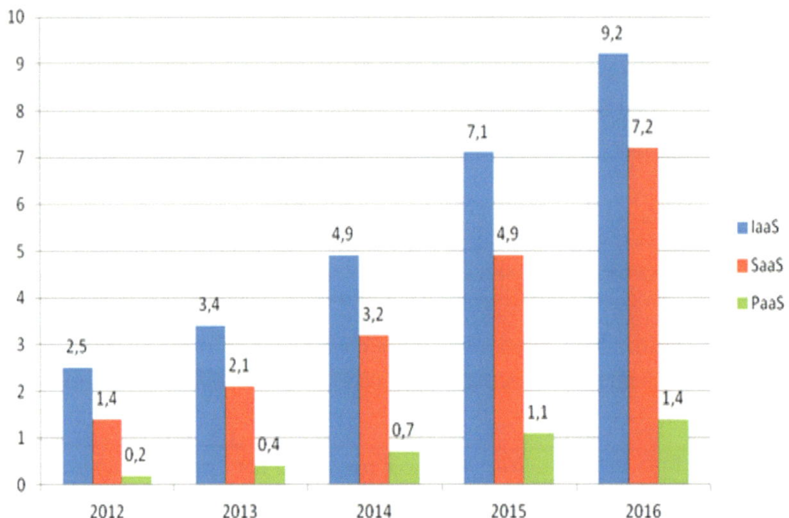

Figure 4. The volume of the Russian cloud technologies market on types of service, billion rubles.

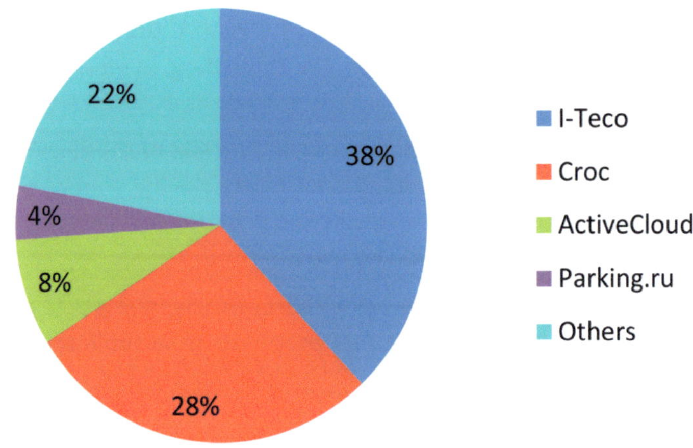

Figure 5. The largest SaaS providers in Russia.

processes as a service) was about 100 million rubles in 2012 each one, and they would make 700 million rubles by 2017 (**Figure 4**) [24, 26].

The preference is given to private clouds in the Russian cloud computing market, because they provide a higher level of safety, allow to integrate easier non-standard decisions, and achieve the best controllability, in comparison with public clouds. In recent years, the designing of hybrid clouds has gained development that is caused by the presence of well-developed IT infrastructure and data-processing centers at many companies. Therefore, the creation of a hybrid cloud is the most appropriate way (**Figure 7**) [32, 33].

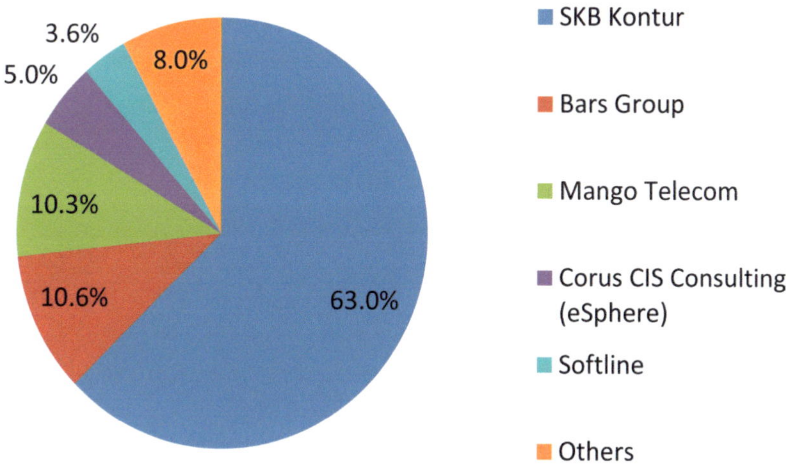

Figure 6. The greatest SaaS service suppliers on the Russian market.

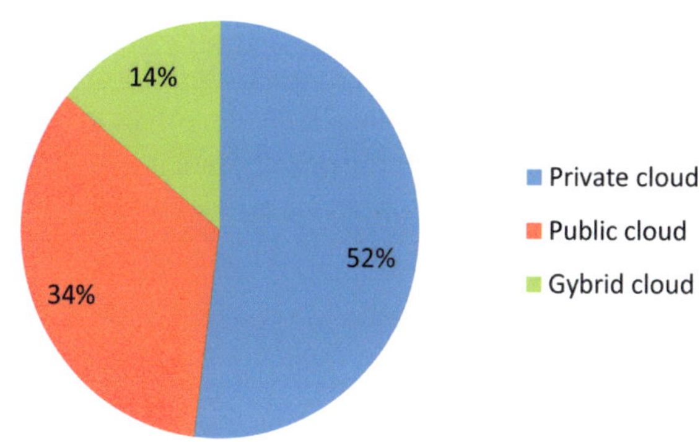

Figure 7. The distribution of cloud types in Russia.

2.6. Cloud computing in the global financial system

Cloud computing becomes more and more demanding for the world financial market. According to the Information Week study, a large number of financial institutions in the world actively use cloud services when running the business. More than 40% of the world financial institutions use software testing as a cloud service, 28% of banks—cloud business applications, 24%—cloud data centers, and 21%—cloud storage (**Figure 8**) [33–38].

In recent years, financial institutions around the world are faced with difficulties in adapting outdated banking systems, launched 20–30 years ago, to modern requirements. Built systems are designed on the basis of a closed architecture, and integration of automated banking systems with new applications is a difficult task, so such solutions are more expensive to use and maintain. In addition, these automated banking systems do not support modern business strategy, because in their heart, the transaction rather than the client.

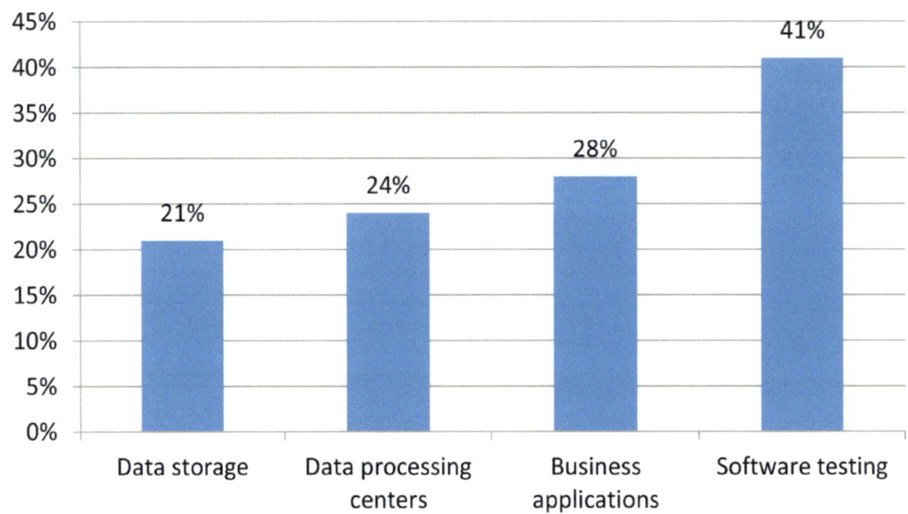

Figure 8. Distribution of cloud services by type of use in financial institutions in the world.

For example, in the United States according to an Aite Group research, more than one-third of banks use ABS older than 16 years and more than half, older than 10 years. A possible replacement of automated banking systems within the next 2 years is called by 13 banks with assets 100–249 million dollars and highly probable 8% of banks with assets between $500 million and 5 billion dollars [39, 40].

Thereby, banks face a choice of implementation, a traditional or cloud automated banking system.

The advantage of cloud automated banking system is the ability to deploy a complete automated banking system on external organization servers, which fully meets the maintenance and configuration of the system, allowing the bank to engage only in the development of business, without going into the features of maintenance and operation of the automation of banking business processes.

The tendency associated with the provision of cloud automated banking systems in financial institutions, in spite of the risks related with the need to ensure the confidentiality of banking information, grows.

Research showed that the introduction of cloud automated banking system goes down in expenses on an average of 20% compared with the conventional automated banking system [39, 40]. This indicator is caused by the following reasons:

- lack of capital costs—no need to spend money for the acquisition of servers and software simultaneously, instead, fixed monthly payments for the rental of equipment and cloud automated banking system are made;
- economy on processes of implementation and technical support of software;
- quick results from the use of the necessary software—no delays related to the implementation;

- the possibility, if necessary, quickly changes the functionality of the system available to a bank;
- a decrease in the number of employees of the IT department, required for interoperability with bank departments' cloud automated banking system;
- absence of expenses for the maintenance of data security; they are placed on servers located in a professionally equipped data center.

As a result of the conducted research of the American banking sector, the Aite Group Company obtained the following results: the cloud used 30% of all US banks in 2006 and about 50% in 2012. According to forecasts, about 90% of all US banks will move to cloud automation systems by 2020 (**Figure 9**) [40].

2.7. Using cloud computing in Russian financial institutions

The use of cloud technologies in the Russian banks did not find such distribution as in the world. There are a number, both objective and subjective, of reasons, for limiting the spread of cloud technologies in the banking sector in Russia.

Firstly, the banks imposed restrictions such as requirements of state regulators in the field of personal data and state secrets and the conditions of the external regulators—the international payment system. All this greatly complicates the transition to cloud computing, especially to hybrid and public clouds.

Secondly, requirements for saving data hold back the development of public cloud technologies. Data security cannot always be provided in public services at the proper level.

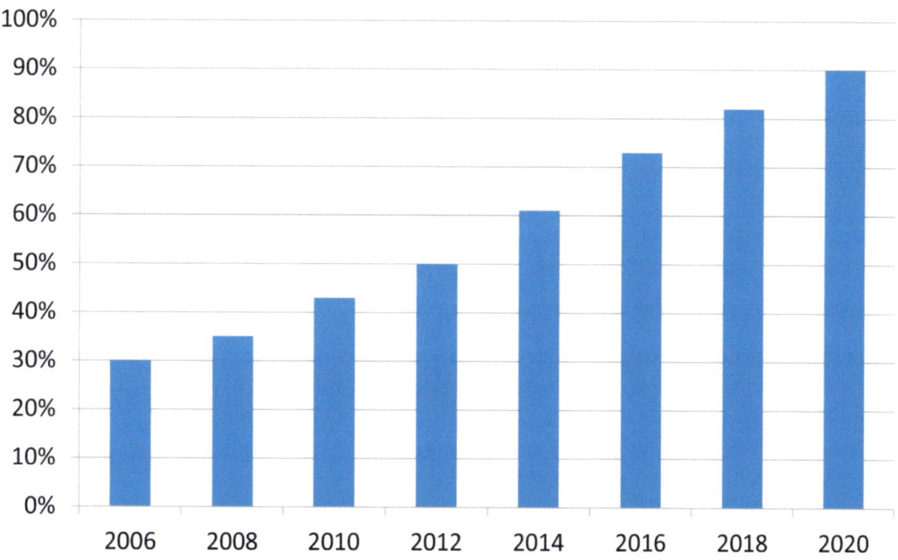

Figure 9. The share of US banks that use the cloud automated banking systems.

Thirdly, the impossibility of self-administration in the clouds is a negative factor for the deployment of cloud services.

Fourthly, the transition to cloud computing requires a significant investment in the restructuring of information infrastructure.

According to a Symantec study among Russian banks, almost three-quarters of respondents are discussing the possibility of moving to the cloud, but most of them have not yet transferred to action. Forty-three percent of respondents expected a sharp increase in the flexibility of IT infrastructure, having been solved on the application of cloud services, but expectations were not fulfilled. In addition, 48% of respondents in vain hoped to improve the efficiency of IT systems, 46% to reduce operating expenses, and 35% to improve safety [23, 28, 30].

These results indicate that the problem is not in the very cloud technologies but an imbalance between what banking institutions expect from these technologies and their real possibilities.

Meanwhile, nowadays, significant changes are traced in the use of financial products because of consumer preferences. In all the banks, remote access to the system of self-service with a warranty of high speed and customer convenience of work was necessary. In addition, the emergence of new financial intermediaries in the market of traditional banking services leads to the growth of competition and the need to find new channels of banks offering their services to customers.

Therefore, in spite of the open questions in the field of security, banks are among the most active consumers of cloud solutions.

Despite the fact that the banks covered their success in using the cloud a little, we can mark several projects of recent years, where cloud technology helped to achieve clear results in terms of efficiency [41–45].

One of the most interesting projects is "Pilot" associated with deploying a private cloud in the Central Bank (the contractor—the company "Jet Infosystems"). A full IaaS platform with a self-service portal was created and used by the means of minimizing the major banking information risks in the cloud. The project result is the considerable increase of processing speed of user requests, greatly reducing the load on the system administration.

Today, global financial business structure, owing to the clouds, may provide services to its offices around the world. For example, the data processing center of "Citibank" in Frankfurt is certified to the highest class and can provide services not only to the western branches of the bank but also to its Russian departments.

PJSC "Sberbank of Russia" also places a high emphasis on the centralization of back-office systems of the territorial banks and introduces the next generation of three-level systems. In the future, the financial institution assumes their transfer to the cloud model.

JSC Gazprombank and PJSC Ak Bars bank are engaged in cloud projects at the present time (the contractor—the ICL-KPO company). JSC Raiffeisenbank positively considers the perspectives of private "cloud" creation for itself. The effective provision of computing power for the solution of specific objectives is the task, which it plans to accomplish in such a way.

JSC "Bank Intesa" is mastering the basic techniques for working with IaaS cloud and tries to use it as a backup data center. The partner is a company "Croc." The bank will examine clouds as one of the main directions of the IT infrastructure development, if cloud technology significantly saves resources and thus the information safety be provided.

The project on transfer in the cloud automated banking system (ABS) appeared in Russia in 2013. "Group of companies CFT" conducts the project in the bank JSC JSCB "International Financial Club." Initially, the bank moved on the use of basic banking applications with cloud technology. Further, the company "Group CFT companies" provided the bank AKB "Moscow Financial Club" cloud ABS, which included not only the virtual computing power but also elements of the security infrastructure, access control, authentication, means to ensure failure, and disaster sustainability. It is expected that the project will enable the bank to cut costs for equipment and maintenance [46–49].

The interest in cloud automated banking systems had been shown in the banking sector in Russia only for the last few years. The only leader in providing cloud technologies is the company "Center of Financial Technologies," which delivers totally automated cloud "CFT-Bank" system, which allows to ensure the comprehensive automation of the entire bank (**Figure 10**).

The first cloud automated banking systems were introduced in the Russian market in 2010 (**Figure 11**).

At the present time, 10 Russian banks introduced cloud platform "CFT-Bank," among them the company "Expobank," JSC "Miraf Bank," JSC "BaykalBank," JSC "International Financial Club," and others.

Any cloud automated banking systems were not implemented in the Russian financial institutions since 2013, and it speaks about the difficult economic situation caused by the

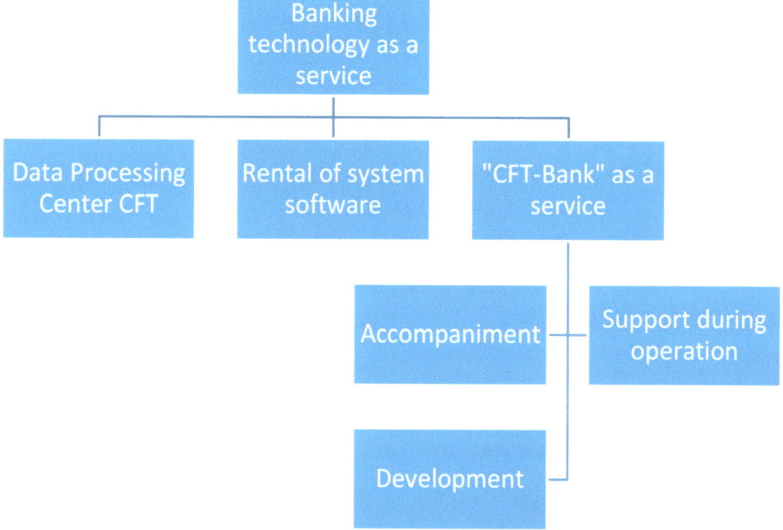

Figure 10. Complex automation of banking services based on cloud computing.

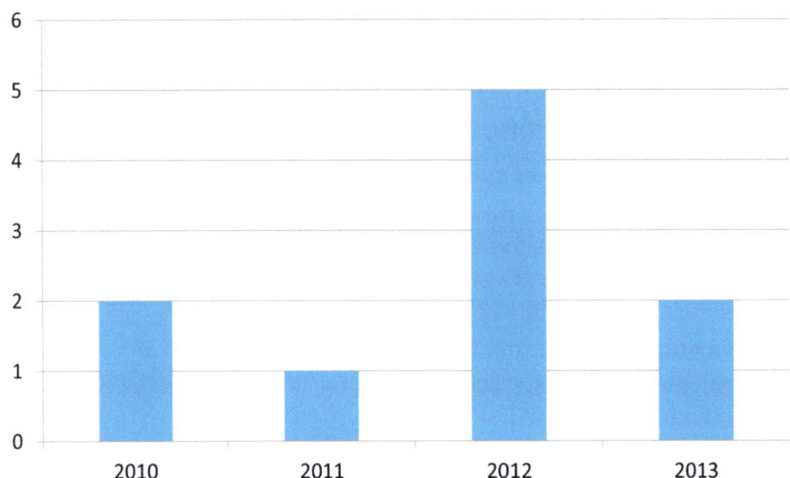

Figure 11. Dynamics of cloud implementations of automated banking systems "CFT-Bank.".

global financial and economic crisis, which led to the closing of major infrastructure projects in the banking sector.

It is possible to achieve considerable cost savings when implementing cloud automated banking system "CFT-Bank" in comparison with the traditional one of the same firm only in one of the parameters associated with a reduction of the number of employees of the IT department. The typical configuration of staff includes 68 people when using the conventional automated banking system; in transition to the cloud automated banking system,

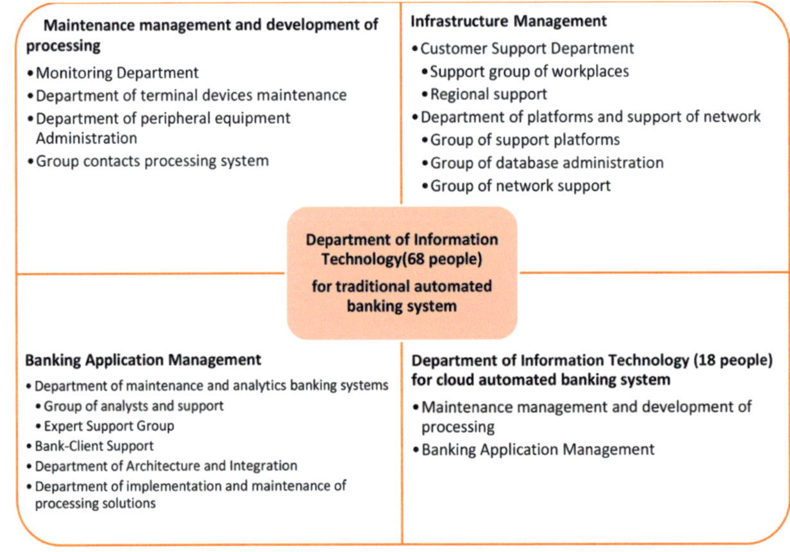

Figure 12. Restructuring of the bank's IT department during the transition to cloud automated banking system of CFT-Bank.

the number of employees can be laid off to 18 people (**Figure 12**), whose main task is to ensure interaction between the departments of the bank with the cloud automated banking system [24, 40, 50–52].

3. Conclusions

In conclusion, the main trends for the implementation of cloud services in the banking system are as follows:

- banks are wary of the use of cloud technology, first of all because of information security;
- implementation of cloud technology takes places in large financial institutions, because the transition requires large investments in the reconfiguration of the bank's IT infrastructure;
- preference will be given to private clouds, capable of providing the required level of information security and the independence of the system configuration; however, the development of hybrid cloud has its perspectives associated with the removal of secondary operations in public clouds;
- the next few years, IaaS model, providing the necessary bank's infrastructure, will develop as cloud technology in the Russian banks; as for SaaS and PaaS models, their development prospects in the financial institutions are unlikely due to the specifics of banking software;
- the use of cloud computing in the field of data storage, data centers, and workplace virtualization is the application of cloud technologies in Russian banks;
- dynamics of cloud services in Russia is ahead of leading indicators by its characteristics in cloud infrastructure an average of 18% per year, and in the cloud services, 30% per year;
- the use of cloud technologies in the banking sector goes in the direction of the use of cloud storage, data centers, business applications, and software testing. There is a tendency of introduction cloud automated banking systems in recent years, which is due to the cost reduction in the implementation compared to conventional ABS, on average 20%;
- introduction of cloud automated banking systems in the Russian financial institutions is slow, only about 1% of Russian banks use cloud ABS.

Author details

Alexey V. Bataev

Address all correspondence to: bat_a68@mail.ru

Higher Engineering and Economics School, Peter the Great St. Petersburg Polytechnic University, St. Petersburg, Russia

References

[1] Bora DK. An Overview of Cloud Computing with Special Reference to Financial Sector. 2011. 117 p

[2] Briggs B, Kassner E. Enterprise Cloud Strategy. Microsoft Press; 2016. 151 p

[3] Dimitrakos T, Martrat J, Wesner S. Service Oriented Infrastructures and Cloud Service Platforms for the Enterprise: A Selection of Common Capabilities Validated in Real-life Business Trials by the BEinGRID Consortium. Springer; 2009. 332 p

[4] Kavis MJ. Architecting the Cloud: Design Decisions for Cloud Computing Service Models (SaaS, PaaS, and IaaS). Wiley; 2014. 224 p

[5] Kondratiev AA. Development of a distributed system security, cloud computing. Software Systems: Theory and Applications. 2011;**4**(8):61-70

[6] Mell P, Grance T. The NIST Definition of Cloud Computing. 2011. NIST Special Publication. 800 p

[7] Smith W. Cloud hosting—A dream come true. Cloud Computing Service. 2011. Available from: www.cloudcomputingservice.html. [Accessed: 2018-01-15]

[8] Vacca J. Cloud Computing Security: Foundations and Challenges. CRC Press; 2016. 518 p

[9] Wortmann H. Business consequences of cloud computing. Innovate IT 2010 Conference; 2010. pp. 91-95

[10] Ghorbel A, Ghorbel M, Jmaiel M. Privacy in cloud computing environments: A survey and research challenges. The Journal of Supercomputing. 2017;**73**(6):2763-2800

[11] Zbakh M, Bakhouya M, Essaaidi M. Cloud computing and big data: Technologies and applications. Concurrency and Computation: Practice and Experience. 2017;**29**(11)

[12] Kaul S, Sood K, Jain A. Cloud computing and its emerging need: Advantages and issues. International Journal of Advanced Research in Computer Science. 2017;**8**(3)

[13] Shirokova EA. Cloud technologies. Modern Trends of Technical Sciences: Proceedings of the International Scientific Conference; 2011. pp. 30-33

[14] Attiya I, Zhang X. Cloud computing technology: Promises and concerns. International Journal of Computer Applications. 2017;**159**(9)

[15] Grebnev E. Cloud services. View from Russia. Moscow: CNews; 2011. 282 p

[16] Chiregi M, Navimipour NJ. Cloud computing and trust evaluation: A systematic literature review of the state-of-the-art mechanisms. Journal of Electrical Systems and Information Technology. 2017

[17] Kshetri N, Fredriksson T, Torres DCR. Big Data and Cloud Computing for Development: Lessons from Key Industries and Economies in the Global South. Taylor & Francis; 2017

[18] Maqueira-Marín JM, Maqueira-Marín JM, Bruque-Cámara S, Bruque-Cámara S, Minguela-Rata B, Minguela-Rata B. Environment determinants in business adoption of cloud computing. Industrial Management & Data Systems. 2017;**117**(1):228-246

[19] Cloud computing (world market). Available from: www.tadviser.ru/index.php [Accessed: 2018-01-15]

[20] Wyld DC. A global look at cloud computing. Language. 2017

[21] Yan Z, Li X, Wang M, Vasilakos A. Flexible data access control based on trust and reputation in cloud computing. IEEE Transactions on Cloud Computing. 2017

[22] News: CIO dissatisfied with the quality of outsourcing services in 2013. Available from: www.cnews.ru/news/top/index.shtml?2013/01/14/515374 [Accessed: 2018-01-15]

[23] Overview: Cloud services in 2012. Available from: www.cnews.ru/reviews/free/cloud/ [Accessed: 2018-01-15]

[24] Overview: Cloud services in 2013. Available from: http://www.cnews.ru/reviews/new/oblachnye_servisy_2013/ [Accessed: 2018-01-15]

[25] Bölöni L, Turgut D. Value of information based scheduling of cloud computing resources. Future Generation Computer Systems. 2017;**71**:212-220

[26] Cloud services (Russian Market). Available from: www.tadviser.ru/index.php [Accessed: 2018-01-15]

[27] Belotserkovskii A. Microsoft Windows Azure: Information. Available from: www.intuit.ru/goods_store/ebooks/9198 [Accessed: 2018-01-15]

[28] Boklacheva EA, Efremov LI. Cloud technologies in Russia: Problems and Prospects. Available from: sisupr.mrsu.ru>2012-1/PDF/14_inf/Boklacheva.pdf [Accessed: 2018-01-15]

[29] Overview: IT in banks and insurance companies in 2012. Available from: www.cnews.ru/reviews/free/banks2012/articles/articles17.shtml [Accessed: 2018-01-15]

[30] Bataev AV. Analysis of cloud technologies use in financial institutions. Actual Problems of Economics. 2015

[31] Bataev AV. Analysis of the use of cloud services and assessment the possibilities of introducing in Russian financial institutions. In: Proceedings of the 29th International Business Information Management Association Conference—Education Excellence and Innovation Management through Vision 2020: From Regional Development Sustainability to Global Economic Growth; 2017

[32] Nikolova L, Rodionov D, Mottaeva A. Securitization of bank assets as a source of financing the innovation activity. International Journal of Economics and Financial Issues. 2016;**T6**(2C):246-252

[33] Aggarwal S. Smart banking–An Introduction: Driven by Information Technology. Vyan Publications; 2016. 175 p

[34] Dummer GW. Banking Automation: Data Processing Systems and Associated Equipment. Pergamon; 2014. 2024 p

[35] Kinsey S, Newton L. International Banking in an Age of Transition: Globalisation, Automation, Banks and Their Archives. Routledge; 2016. 216 p

[36] Reed J. FinTech: Financial Technology and Modern Finance in the 21st Century. 2016. 50 p

[37] Shah M, Clarke S. E-Banking Management: Issues, Solutions, and Strategies, Information Science Reference. 2009. 310 p

[38] Sunami KY. Ubiquitous banks: Cloud based design for core banking. International Journal. 2017;**8**(2)

[39] Ke MT, Yeh CH, Su CJ. Cloud computing platform for real-time measurement and verification of energy performance. Applied Energy. 2017;**188**:497-507

[40] Dawes CG. The Banking System of the United States and Its Relation to the Money and Business of the Country. Forgotten Books. 2012. 90 p

[41] Outsourcing ABS–A recognized need. Banking Review. Available from: bosfera.ru/bo/2013/07/autsorsing-abs [Accessed: 2018-01-16]

[42] Narter B. Banking in the Cloud. 2011. Available from: www.temenos.com. [Accessed: 2018-01-16]

[43] Rafaels RJ. Cloud Computing: From Beginning to End. CreateSpace Independent Publishing Platform; 2015. 152 p

[44] Ruiter J, Warnier M. Privacy regulations for cloud computing: Compliance and implementation in theory and practice. In: Computers, Privacy and DataProtection: An Element of Choice. 2011. pp. 361-376

[45] Sriram S. Cloud Computing in Banking, 2010. 284 p

[46] Automated banking system: The cost. Available from: www.absonline.ru/software/cost/ [Accessed: 2018-01-15]

[47] Ruparelia NB. Cloud Computing. The MIT Press; 2016. 280 p

[48] Sangameswar S. Cloud Computing–An Introduction. 2015. 30 p

[49] Bruin B, Floridi L. The ethics of cloud computing. Science and Engineering Ethics. 2017;**23**(1):21-39

[50] Lee YC. Adoption Intention of Cloud Computing at the Firm Level. Journal of Computer Information Systems. 2017:1-12

[51] Varghese B, Buyya R. Next generation cloud computing: New trends and research directions. Future Generation Computer Systems. 2017;**79**:849-861

[52] CFT. The Structure of Cloud Services. M.: CFT; 2013. 36 p